FAMOUS ATHLETES

Pebble®

LEBRON JAMES

by Tracy Nelson Maurer

Gail Saunders-Smith, PhD, Consulting Editor

CAPSTONE PRESS
a capstone imprint

Pebble Books are published by Capstone Press,
1710 Roe Crest Drive, North Mankato, Minnesota 56003
www.capstonepub.com

Library of Congress Cataloging-in-Publication Data
Maurer, Tracy, 1965–
  LeBron James / by Tracy Nelson Maurer.
    pages cm.—(Pebble Books. Famous athletes)
  Includes bibliographical references and index.
ISBN 978-1-4914-6236-2 (library binding : alk. paper)
ISBN 978-1-4914-6252-2 (ebook pdf)
ISBN 978-1-4914-6256-0 (pebble books pbk. : alk. paper)
1. James, LeBron—Juvenile literature. 2. Basketball players—United States—
Biography—Juvenile literature. I. Title.
  GV865.T73M38 2016
  796.357092—dc23
  [B]   2015001900

Note to Parents and Teachers

The Famous Athletes supports national curriculum standards for
social studies related to people, places, and culture. This book
describes and illustrates LeBron James. The images support early
readers in understanding the text. The repetition of words and
phrases helps early readers learn new words. This book also
introduces early readers to subject-specific vocabulary words,
which are defined in the Glossary section. Early readers may need
assistance to read some words and to use the Table of Contents,
Glossary, Read More, Internet Sites, and Index sections of the book.

Printed in the United States of America.
032019   000068

TABLE OF CONTENTS

1984

born in
Akron, Ohio

4

LOVING THE GAME

LeBron Raymone James has always loved basketball. He was born December 30, 1984. Even as a baby, LeBron played with a toy basketball every day.

1984

born in
Akron, Ohio

1994

lives with the
Frank Walker
family for the
next two years

LeBron's mother, Gloria, raised him by herself. They moved often. LeBron almost quit sports after fourth grade. Then in 1994 a coach asked LeBron to live with his family in Akron, Ohio.

 8

1984
born in
Akron, Ohio

1994
lives with the
Frank Walker
family for the
next two years

**1999–
2003**
attends
St. Vincent–
St. Mary
High School

HIGH SCHOOL STAR

By 10th grade LeBron was

6 feet, 7 inches (2 meters) tall.

He stood out as a star

on his high school football

and basketball teams.

1984
born in
Akron, Ohio

1994
lives with the
Frank Walker
family for the
next two years

**1999–
2003**
attends
St. Vincent–
St. Mary
High School

LeBron made great shots.

He passed the basketball well.

LeBron ruled the court.

Fans called him "King James."

1984
born in
Akron, Ohio

1994
lives with the
Frank Walker
family for the
next two years

**1999–
2003**
attends
St. Vincent–
St. Mary
High School

2003
drafted
by the
Cleveland
Cavaliers

NBA SUPERSTAR

After high school LeBron was the top pick in the 2003 NBA Draft. The Cleveland Cavaliers chose him. LeBron was happy. He would play for his home state's team.

NBA stands for National Basketball Association.

1984
born in
Akron, Ohio

1994
lives with the
Frank Walker
family for the
next two years

**1999–
2003**
attends
St. Vincent–
St. Mary
High School

2003
drafted
by the
Cleveland
Cavaliers

The Cavaliers became

a better team with LeBron.

He helped them win

more games than

in past seasons.

1984	1994	1999–2003	2003
born in Akron, Ohio	lives with the Frank Walker family for the next two years	attends St. Vincent– St. Mary High School	drafted by the Cleveland Cavaliers

After seven years,

the Cavaliers still had not

won a NBA championship.

LeBron left Cleveland to play

for the Miami Heat in Florida.

2010

joins the
Miami Heat

1984	1994	1999–2003	2003
born in Akron, Ohio	lives with the Frank Walker family for the next two years	attends St. Vincent–St. Mary High School	drafted by the Cleveland Cavaliers

LeBron and the Miami Heat
played in the NBA Finals
each year between 2011
and 2014. LeBron was named
the Finals MVP in both 2012
and 2013.

2010

joins the
Miami Heat

2012–2013

Miami Heat win
back-to-back
championships

MVP stands for
Most Valuable Player.

1984
born in
Akron, Ohio

1994
lives with the
Frank Walker
family for the
next two years

1999–2003
attends
St. Vincent–
St. Mary
High School

2003
drafted
by the
Cleveland
Cavaliers

BACK HOME

LeBron returned to the
Cleveland Cavaliers in 2014.
He had a great season
playing for his home team.
LeBron led them all the way
to the NBA Finals.

2010
joins the
Miami Heat

2012-2013
Miami Heat win
back-to-back
championships

2014
returns to the
Cleveland Cavaliers

GLOSSARY

court—the hard surface on which a basketball game is played

draft—an event held for teams to choose new people to play for them

NBA Finals—the games that decide the season's championship

season—the time of year in which NBA basketball games are played

CRITICAL THINKING
USING THE COMMON CORE

1. Why do fans call LeBron "King James"? (Key Ideas and Details)

2. What is one reason LeBron may have returned to the Cavaliers in 2014? (Integration of Knowledge and Ideas)

READ MORE

Ciovacco, Justine. *LeBron James: NBA Champion.* Living Legends of Sports. New York: Rosen Publishing, 2015.

Doeden, Matt. *Stars of Basketball.* Sports Stars. North Mankato, Minn.: Capstone Press, 2014.

Nagelhout, Ryan. *I Love Basketball.* My Favorite Sports. New York: Gareth Stevens Publishing, 2015.

INTERNET SITES

FactHound offers a safe, fun way to find Internet sites related to this book. All of the sites on FactHound have been researched by our staff.

Here's all you do:

Visit *www.facthound.com*

Type in this code: 9781491462362

Check out projects, games and lots more at
www.capstonekids.com

23

INDEX

Word Count: 226
Grade: 1
Early-Intervention Level: 18

Editorial Credits
Erika L. Shores, editor; Juliette Peters, designer;
Eric Gohl, media researcher; Lori Barbeau, production specialist

Photo Credits
AP Photo: Tony Dejak, cover; Newscom: Icon SMI/Bob Falcetti, 8, KRT/Ed Suba
Jr., 10, 12, KRT/Phil Masturzo, 6, Reuters/Mike Blake, 14, Reuters/Mike Ehrmann,
16, Reuters/Mike Segar, 18, USA Today Sports/David Richard, 1, 4, 20

Design Elements: Shutterstock

milk,
sulphate,
and alby starvation

martin millar

Soft Skull Press
Brooklyn

Other Books by Martin Millar

Lonely Werewolf Girl
The Good Fairies of New York
Suzy, Led Zeppelin, and Me
Lux the Poet

Jesus Christ what a fucking wreck I am, my face looks a hundred years old, people would scream if I went out on the streets, my hair's all falling out, there's a woman from the Milk Marketing Board trying to kill me. She learns my address, that's it, I'm dead.

So I'm sitting taping David Rodigan's reggae show from the radio and plotting how to sell my comics without getting killed. With capital from the comics I can buy studio time to make a record which will be just great, or else buy a gun to kill the woman who's got the contract on me. Also with a gun I could take militant steps to corner the sulphate market in Brixton. I mean, just because that man who threatened me was Chinese doesn't mean he was from a Triad, does it? I'm not scared of him, I mean, why would a Triad be interested in the minimal profit in Brixton sulphate?

All over this flat there are mirrors, big, small, in every position. I'm trying to avoid them.

There's a Chinese man walking confidently around Soho. Actually he comes from Hong Kong. He's buying food and looking round at the sunshine and giving some small thought to some business he has in south London. Mostly though he's just walking round being pleased with himself.

I could sit here all night.

Forever.

I got a pain in my guts.

Maybe it would go away if I ate something but I don't want to get fat. If someone came visiting maybe I could get a cigarette off them, I've given up smoking and it's so fucking boring I don't want to talk about it.

I didn't mean to aggravate the Milk Marketing Board, I mean, I never wanted all that publicity in the first place. I was just trying to be helpful. How was I to know they would end up with their poorest ever May sales figures since they began keeping records?

I was really ill some time ago. I don't want to imply that I'm well now, just that then I was a lot worse.

My doctor really loathes me. Every time I go to see him he talks to me with open contempt, he's putting on a front that he thinks I'm a hypochondriac but really he knows I'm sick and he enjoys seeing me suffer. Upper-class bastard, what's he doing being a doctor in this area if he hates us? Bastard.

June was trained by the Brazilian secret police and now she works in Britain as a hired killer. She has a one hundred percent success record and a good reputation for discretion. That is, no one ever sees her killing her target, no one ever knows anything about her work and no one finds more than a corpse with a bullet in it, well sometimes more than one bullet, she's not a purist and doesn't mind pumping in a few if it seems necessary. But generally she shoots her victim with a silenced automatic in some quiet place and everything is fine for all concerned, for her, for her client and for her booking agent.

At this moment she is cutting her hair in front of a small mirror on the kitchen table. She always cuts her own hair and she does it well but if she made a mistake and ended up with some hideously uneven mess it wouldn't trouble her too much.

She doesn't have to kill people all that often because the pay is good and she is not greedy. She has never worked for the Milk Marketing Board before.

Well, selling these comics is a formidable task because for one thing there are an awful lot of them and short of hiring a truck, which I can't afford, how am I going to get them up to the comic shop? And when I do get them there (Why won't that wretched fucker in the shop come down here and value them? Not that I'd tell him my address anyway in case that hitwoman tortured him to find it out. But he won't come anyway.) how do I know that they won't try to rip me off? Bastards.

I mean, my comics are worth thousands of pounds but if the owner of the shop knows I'm desperate for money he's bound to make me some cheap offer, I'll take them off your hands as a friendly gesture, that sort of thing. Maybe I could threaten him with my gun. No, I can't get the gun till I get the money from selling the comics.

I could check the prices in the trade book but I don't know if the general public are allowed to look at it. And there is always the possibility that the shop might only want to buy a selected few of my collection and I'm sure not going to all this trouble hiring trucks to get up there and back and then them only buying a few, bastards. I can tell already that I'm gonna get done, I can sense these things coming. This comic shop owner better watch out or he's gonna end up with a bullet in his back.

Maybe I could hold up the comic shop instead and steal their valuable comics. That would teach them a lesson.

I like comics, especially *Conan* and *Spiderman*.

The Chinese man is a fairly mysterious character, and not just because he's Chinese. At one time he was involved in heroin quality control in the southern corner of the Golden Triangle in Burma.

After a power struggle in which the warlord he served was mown down along with his still loyal bodyguards, he fled through Thailand, Cambodia, and Vietnam into Australia and from there to the United States. All the way through he bought his safety out of the vast profits he'd made in the heroin industry.

He had friends in the USA but he didn't stay. He moved to Britain, for reasons that are not clear.

Now he pretends to earn his living by teaching Chinese. But in reality he has only one pupil and even she is an employee of his. He earns his money from illegal activities. The teaching Chinese is a front to fool investigative reporters. In between his origins in Hong Kong and his work in Burma he learned Wing Chun kung fu and he is deadly efficient in its practice.

He has contacts and family friends in London. Much drug trade goes through him already, much profitable and important business.

He is anxious to get in touch with a small-time sulphate dealer in Brixton.

The speakers on the record player don't work properly, or maybe it's the amplifier that doesn't work, anyway the bass won't come over loud enough and how can I play reggae if the bass won't come over loud enough?

Wha this.

Wha that.

Papa Sinbad a chat.

An' me nice up the area murderer!

An' the roots an' culture murderer!

This poverty is real suffering you know, nothing in the flat works and I look about a hundred and fifty. If I was rich or even well off I wouldn't look so old, rich people never seem to look so bad when they get old. How did I get to be twenty-six anyway? I mean, what happened?

Imagine getting injured somehow and your skull is split open and you have to hold it together till help arrives and if you take your hands away from your head it falls apart. I'd hate that.

In Leeds there is a chemical explosion in a Boots factory. There is no danger to local residents but police advise car owners to wash their cars as a precaution and I'm waiting with interest to see what gruesome deformities result.

I was really ill a while ago, I was going blind and my skin was fading into a washed-up yellow long-dead-vegetation colour.

Every time I got an attack my eyes would close up a little more and my skin would shrink and fade, I'd stumble and crawl down the road to the doctor, hurting inside where my organs were straining to get out and he'd look me straight in my puffed-up mixamatosis face and tell me I was suffering from nerves.

"But doctor," I'd croak, "my insides are fighting to get out and my skin looks like an old newspaper and my left eye has completely closed up and there's blood seeping out of the right one and I haven't been able to keep down food for four days and I feel sick even when I get better."

"That's all right, it's just your nerves, I see lots like you." He'd look at me in contempt.

"But I'm going blind."

"Learn to relax."

Next time I get a bad attack I go back. The receptionist reels in horror when she sees me. I stagger into the doctor's room and collapse onto the floor and start sobbing and whimpering.

He prescribes me some valium. He writes the prescription like he's never wasted so much time in his whole life.

I wonder if I'll be reincarnated after this crazed gun-woman shoots me, I'd be dead already if I hadn't got that tip-off. I wish I could be reincarnated with my memories intact, in which case I could probably manage my life instead of completely fucking it up, lie in a cot for a couple of years with nothing to do but plan out my strategy for when I start to walk.

I'm going round taking the polythene off the windows in case I have to make a quick escape. I don't know if it kept the heat in but it sure made a lot of noise. Anyway I don't want this killer bursting in waving a meat axe or machine gun or whatever she's going to do the business with and me trying to fling myself out of the window in one last desperate bid for freedom and bouncing back off the securely-stuck-on seasonal double-glazing.

Perhaps I should move again. But what would I do about my comics?

Down in Brixton the youth are shambling through the streets wondering where their next drug is coming from. The sun is shining and nobody seems too troubled by anybody else and through the market music pulses out of many record shacks and the atmosphere is generally that of being quite a nice place to live.

Fran and Julie like living here, they share the lower floor of a reasonable squat with a front door like Fort Knox and a million cats but quite a lot of drugs around with some food in between and hair dye in brilliant colours no trouble to get and music everywhere and a good cinema that doesn't spend all its time showing meathead films, a women's self-defence class, the dole office close by, poverty but isn't everyone. Not a bad life right now. Fran picks at a guitar and wonders where Alby Starvation is, he ought to have arrived with their speed by now.

What a fucking pain, she thinks, if I have to go on stage tonight without speeding, I'll never manage it, I wonder if anyone in the street's got any food?

In the next room Julie practices self-defence, aiming knee-high kicks at a chair. Smash someone in the knee, her instructor tells her, and they won't want to bother you again for a while.

This is good advice providing you don't miscalculate because then they will really be mad and kill you.

Julie practices against the chair.

So there I was getting sicker and sicker and my pig of a doctor, a misnomer if ever there was one, deliberately refused to help me.

At the time I'm wondering if he's got some ulterior motive like maybe he's in league with the Chinese man from Soho. Or maybe he's after my comics, that's it, he's probably secretly craving for my *Silver Surfer* No. 1 and hopes to get his hands on it after I'm dead, probably along the lines of representations to the executor of my estate, I cared for him all through the years of his terrible illness, don't auction his *Silver Surfer* collection, give them to me like he promised. Bastard.

One thing, though, I always make some sort of recovery from these bouts of illness, usually after passing out and waking up covered in vomit. I'm feeling a lot better, I drink some water and rest a while, wipe the blood from my eyes and ears and start to feel a bit like a human being. I manage a smile for the hamster, my only friend.

It never lasted though, as soon as I got better I got worse and it was always a little bit more unpleasant than the last time. Nobody's skin was ever that colour, it was ridiculous.

What a miserable time. I still feel bad thinking about it.

And now I'm sitting here in comparative health and fear. Tomorrow I intend to wing my way down to Brixton and deliver some sulphate to a few people for some pathetically small profit and I wonder why I do it particularly as half of China seems to be hot on my trail for god knows what reason and anyway I just seem to take most of it myself.

Two people of my acquaintance have been approached by this Chinese man, who gave them a close description of me and knew my name and displayed a disconcerting knowledge of my activities, asking where he could find me. Both of them lied, of course, and said they didn't know. What if he comes back and threatens them?

Look, why are all these people trying to kill me? What have I ever done to them? OK, so I don't have actual proof that this fiend of an oriental is trying to kill me but as it seems to be the norm these days I can only presume the worst.

Maybe he does belong to a Triad. Maybe I insulted them somehow, I got a comic that says that's a pretty bad thing to do. He wants to take over my business, I can tell. Bastard, why doesn't he leave me alone with my misery. Wait till I get a gun, I'll show them.

I'm tired. I'm gonna make a peanut butter and marmite sandwich and go to bed. I'm gonna barricade, bolt, and booby trap my bedroom door as protection from this woman from the Milk Marketing Board who's out to get me.

My guts hurt.

So why not ask your doctor to send you to hospital said one of my friends eventually.

It seems like a good idea so I go down painfully to the surgery when the next attack comes on and bleed a bit on the carpet. This doctor has a vile face and a voice like an old BBC newscaster.

"The hospital? But you'll be wasting your time, it's just your nerves."

I threaten to kill him there and then. He agrees to give me a letter to take to the hospital.

I drag myself down. In the street people are looking askance at my horribly diseased features. Shoppers cross the road to avoid me and small children start to cry as I pass. The wind blows and it feels like it's going to carry me away.

At the hospital I wait for hours and hours while the nurses whisper and talk about me behind my back. It seems to me that they must have shuffled my card to the bottom of the pile.

When they do tests and things they have the nerve to tell me there is nothing wrong.

Of course, I should have realised that these medical people would all stick together and that probably my doctor didn't write anything at all about my appalling symptoms in his letter but just a note saying they were to let me die so he could get his hands on my *Silver Surfer* No. 1.

By this time I'm almost completely blind and I'm hurting so much inside I can hardly bear to move.

All right, I think, I don't need them. I'll cure myself.

June has finished cutting her hair and her thoughts turn to her current contract. She has to kill some person in Brixton. He is called Alby Starvation. She does not know his address, which is unusual in her line of work, but he has moved recently and seems to be in hiding. But she knows she will find him easily enough. Taking her gun casually out of a drawer in the kitchen she sits down to clean it whilst eating some cereal. Tomorrow she hopes to complete the contract. She thinks briefly of her training in Brazil.

Fran wanders out to steal some food from Big Value stores.

The manager of Big Value is a bitter man. His career is stymied because his cat died of cancer. He knows that senior management don't trust him any more and won't promote him to a bigger store, how could we promote a man whose cat died of cancer? If he couldn't look after a cat properly what would he do with a major branch of Big Value?

Fran stuffs food into her pockets and leaves the shop. She smiles at the security guard. The security guard has other things on his mind.

Some reggae music floats past *chuka chuka chuka* as Fran drifts down the road with pockets full of food. Fran has cropped skinhead hair, mostly black with traces of green here and there. It never occurs to her that she might be caught stealing and she never is.

Tonight her band is playing a gig in a small hall close by, which is no big deal but might be fun or then again might not. Fran plays bass guitar, not very well but well enough.

She goes home to share her food with Julie. Julie completely lacks her talent for acquiring provisions though she is better at fighting.

John Peel plays a request for someone. It is a good record but I forget what it is. Well, how did it come about that they sent this killer after me?

I'm sick and dying (this is about six months ago), things are looking serious, the hamster looks concerned.

The roof of my flat is dirty white and scarred, it's repaired in three places, the results of past burglaries. People break into the communal loft that runs along the top of the block, walk over, then smash their way through the ceilings of the top-floor flats. I've not lived here for very long and I am constantly awaiting the arrival of a gang of thugs through my ceiling, probably as I sleep. They might only intend to burgle the flat but when they find me here they will kill me in some brutal fashion. They will have to kill me in case I identify them later. Even though I promise to keep my mouth shut, to not even call the police, they will still kill me because the leader of the gang is a sadistic monster who enjoys inflicting pain on nature's victims. Bastards, why don't you leave me alone?

Anyway, my illness is reaching terminal proportions when one day I get a visitor, Stacey, a friend.

I tell him about my terrible sickness and amazingly he comes up with a sensible suggestion.

"You're probably allergic to something in your diet. I read about it somewhere. It said that people often get mystery illnesses that baffle medical science and all the time it's due to hidden allergies."

"Well, how can I find out before I die?" I enquire.

"You go on a fast," he tells me. "Clear out your system for five days, then start eating one food at a time, like one day is only brown rice for instance, and a few days later you add something else like lettuce, and if you keep healthy then these foods are OK. But when you add something and some hours later you start vomiting and bleeding and things, well, then you've pinpointed the problem."

I thank him profusely and begin my five-day fast.

After she left Brazil, June travelled through Mexico into the USA. She didn't like the people much.

One night in a cocktail bar a man tries to pick her up. She tries discouraging him politely but he keeps pestering her so eventually she tells him to go fuck himself.

Later that night when she arrives home her trained senses tell her that there is something wrong. As she puts the key in the door of the flat she is renting she hears a sound and spins round and there is the man who was troubling her in the bar. What is more he has a friend with him.

This puts June momentarily off her stride, the friend being another man, and before she can react they push her through the door. Both men are slightly drunk and they are both large and neither of them has anything but malice apparent.

Without saying anything the man who spoke to her in the bar reaches out to grab her breast but by now June's training is taking over. She already feels annoyed that it has momentarily deserted her. She blocks his hand and smashes the side of her palm into his windpipe. Almost simultaneously she stamps a brutal kick into his knee. He gurgles and falls down.

June spins to face the other man and whips in to attack. She is so quick that her blow would have landed on almost anyone but a former US Marine trained in man-to-man combat which is just what her second assailant is. Moving with abnormal speed he neutralises June's attack. (Later, June wonders if her speed was fractionally impaired by some slight inhibition. She has never had to fight in earnest before.)

The man takes out a knife and drops into what looks like a trained knife-fighter's stance. June knows how to defend herself against a knife attack with her bare hands.

But instead she pulls out her gun and shoots him dead because, all in all, it seems like a reasonable thing to do. The first man gropes his way off the floor and she shoots him as well.

She packs her bag and leaves for Europe.

So I took Stacey's advice and began my five-day fast.

Well, after fasting for a few days I'm feeling better already. I mean, I feel like I'm starving to death but that's an improvement. My blindness has almost completely gone and it's nice to see again. The pains are leaving my insides. My skin is still a disgusting colour but you can't expect miracles.

Well, I've got through another night without being killed in my bed by burglars but now comes the difficult part, I got to step outside and down to Brixton and no doubt there's a telescopic sight trained on my door at this very moment as well as a horde of Chinese with knives on the landing below but nevertheless I have to go, I got sulphate deliveries to make and what's more I got no food in the house and I hate to go hungry.

And also I have to make enquiries about hiring some sort of transport to move my comics uptown to sell them, and also I have to make enquiries about where to buy a gun, something I'm not quite sure how you go about. And once you get one is it hard to shoot? How do you learn? I mean, it's all right if you're in the Mafia or something and the family owns a couple of shooting ranges, no trouble at all, you just go down there with an instructor and blast away in between ice-pick training and develop the skill, but how could I learn to shoot? It's not legal to go out and practice in the park, besides I might hurt someone, most likely myself.

Right now there is a big Mafia trial in Italy. When you get to be a real big-time criminal you no longer have to shoot people and you become indistinguishable from an accountant.

Well, here comes the Fall. Not many bands sound like the Fall, give them hell, Mark.

I'm walking down to Brixton.

I'm practicing my 360-degree vision.

I'm listening for the slightest sound of a killer.

Every sense is working overtime.

My nerves are suffering acute downpression.

It's fucking miserable.

The Chinese man has just finished some business and is now eating some steak and chips in a restaurant. His car is waiting nearby with his driver-cum-bodyguard. The driver reads a newspaper and thinks about a video game he wants to buy. He's been playing this game around the arcades, but Wu, his arch rival, keeps beating him. So Cheng, the driver, plans to buy the game module and do some heavy practising at home.

After this secret practice he'll go out and blitz Wu in the arcade.

Their struggle for supremacy in the video game stakes in Soho is a long-time affair and victory in any one game can never be conclusive, but Cheng feels that if he can come from behind and unexpectedly rout Wu then it will be a significant psychological blow in his favour and may well cause his opponent to crumble.

Wu and Cheng used to be good friends but their rivalry over the games has poisoned their relationship. Now when they meet they swap insincere smiles and head for the machines. People recognise them and flock around to watch their contests, for the constant practice has made them formidable players and they could easily defeat any of the other players in the arcades.

They stand or sit, depending on the machine, faces fixed in serious frowns, minds rooted in deepest concentration as the coloured lights flicker over the screen.

They never play for fun any more.

The Chinese man leaves the restaurant and walks the short distance to his car. It is parked illegally but is in no danger of getting a parking ticket or having its wheel clamped because part of his web of crime and intrigue involves bribing the local police and traffic wardens. Traffic wardens are not often bribed but the Chinese man is very thorough and really can't be bothered getting parking tickets and wheel clamps every time he wants to park in Soho.

They head down to Brixton.

Trouble you a trouble me, yes I, awoh, a jus flash it!

The rhythm pumps out of the little rasta's ghetto blaster, a gigantic portable cassette recorder more or less the same size as him. The rasta is short and his locks are wrapped up inside a big brown hat. I'm walking down the hill behind him, deliberately not passing so I can listen to the music.

Well after I'd fasted for five days all of my symptoms had gone except for my jaundiced colour and I hoped that might just be the result of malnutrition.

Even the hunger has gone and I'm feeling better than I have for months, in fact I seem to be floating.

The only problem is that now I have to eat and I wonder what to start with. Yoghurt? I eat lots of yoghurt. I eat so much fucking yoghurt it's coming out my fucking ears. Brown rice? Carrots? A Mars bar? It has to be something pure so I decide on brown rice. It tastes dull but then its yin and yang are perfectly balanced.

So with some trepidation I cook brown rice and when it comes to it I can only manage a few mouthfuls, five days not eating I guess my stomach's shrunk pretty small by now. I wait to get ill again, all day waiting for my eyes to blacken, swell, and close, my organs to start fighting each other, but nothing happens. OK, rice is fine. I begin to feel that my death may not be imminent.

I tell all my friends about the process and they are all fascinated. "We're rooting for you," they say.

After a week I'm eating lettuce, carrots, and rice and I'm bored but healthy.

I celebrate by buying some records from Desmond Hip City and when I get home I dance and don't worry too much that the bass on the record player isn't working too well. I try giving up smoking and fail immediately.

Nevermind.

I'm walking down to Fran and Julie's.

Down the hill an old couple sit on their balcony like they always do and they wave to me like they always do. I wave back and shout a greeting and if times were not so dangerous I'd stay for a talk, this poor couple I guess they get to talk to about one person a week. So they spend their time on the balcony, looking out.

It's not safe for me to hang around here, however. It's not really safe for me to hang around anywhere in Britain. Staying in London is suicidal but if I leave then all these predators will get their hands on my comics and I can't bear the thought.

I pass people going about their normal daily business. This depresses me more than anything.

This big plane flies overhead and it roars and spits and drowns out the music walking in front of me. I don't look up because the only thing that flies over London making such a racket is a Concorde. This has been flying over and about for many years now and is still a constant source of annoyance to me. It should give me a warm feeling inside to think of all those businessmen getting quickly from here to there and oiling the wheels of industry to the ultimate benefit of those such as me but it doesn't.

How come I got black lines under my eyes? No one else seems to get them so bad, not even people who abuse themselves to a considerable degree. I get the least bit tired and big black shadows appear like magic and this is just one more instance of life's constant picking on me.

It's sunshine in Brixton.

The Chinese man reaches Brixton and to his surprise immediately spots the person he is looking for. He tells Cheng to pull up and they glide to a halt. The Chinese man winds down the window.

God there's a car pulling up they've found me already. It's the Chinese, the ones that've been looking for me, I can see two of them, one of them looks vicious as hell. I panic and try to run but my poor frightened body won't respond. The window winds down and I wait for the muzzle of a machine gun to poke me in the ribs before cutting me in half.

It does not materialise and I realise that they are going to take me away and torture me.

"I've been looking for you," says the Chinese man in the most sinister voice this side of Lon Chaney.

I manage to croak, "What do you want?"

"I have something to say to you in private. Is there somewhere that we could speak for a little while?"

I look around for the best direction for flight and test my legs to see if the paralysis has gone. Not quite. If I can just stall for a few seconds before they drag me off I'll make a break for it. Chinese tortures are pretty grim. There doesn't feel like there's enough room in my mouth to hold all of my tongue. Another black thought emerges.

"Are you from the Milk Marketing Board as well?" I demand. He looks puzzled, or pretends to. "Or are you just after my sulphate business? I've got friends you know, I'm pretty close to the Mafia in Britain, my mother comes from Naples."

He's about to speak but a policeman wanders into view and I take advantage of this to make a brave bid for freedom. I'm flying down the street waiting for a bullet in the back or possibly a shuriken throwing star but by a miracle I reach the corner of the road unpunctured. I get round it like an Olympic sprinter and collide head on with a young girl. We tumble to the ground. Watch where you're going, I scream in rage and fear and shove her out the way. I risk a glance over my shoulder and though several people are looking with interest at my fleeing figure, none of them appear to be Chinese.

My terror keeps me going strong till I reach the house of Fran and Julie. I trip in the path and beat on the door with my head, let me in they're trying to torture me, I wail.

The door opens when I'm still on my knees and I crawl thankfully inside.

"Hide me Fran, that Chinese person has found me."

"What did he do?"

"He tried to kill me."

"Did you bring the amphetamines?"

The manager of Big Value is extremely upset because he has just got the figures from the latest stocktake and they reveal that an incredible amount of merchandise has gone missing through shoplifting.

He takes it out on the chief security guard. The chief security guard loathes the manager and in reality would be fairly pleased at the stock loss were it not for the fact that it reflects so badly on him. The manager is incensed and gives him a hard time.

"When was the last time you actually caught anyone shoplifting, you useless bastard? How is it possible that thieves walked out with two gas fires and a kitchen table? The store is always crawling with degenerates, how come you never catch any of them?"

For fuck's sake, thinks the chief security guard, what's he going on at me for, I only stand around in a uniform organising things, there's other people here supposed to be catching them as well.

Later the manager is in deep gloom. His career is tumbling before his eyes, he suffers not only the contempt of his colleagues over his diseased cat (Whoever heard of a cat getting cancer of the throat? What had he been doing to it?) but also extreme disapproval from head office over the figures he has been sending in. Why did everyone come and steal out of his store for Christ's sake? Why couldn't they go some other place and plague someone else?

He hated Brixton, full of lesbian feminists and punks and rastas and communists and any other filthy degenerate you care to name, all of them wearing appalling old ripped up second-hand clothing with their hair in bizarre cuts and colours and stealing benefits from the state hand over fist.

How come he doesn't work in some nice suburban area like his cousin? His cousin manages a store as well but he isn't constantly plagued with lowlife clientele.

The Chinese man drives the streets, still looking.

It's a few days later in the allergy test. I'm up to seven separate items I can eat without dying and I'm trying an eighth, a glass of milk.

A half-hour after I've drunk it I feel dizzy and my vision blurs. I look in a mirror and there's blood seeping out from under one eyelid. Inside me things begin to churn. I throw up and keep throwing up long after my stomach is empty. As I'm gasping for breath and trying not to irritate my red puffy eyes it strikes me that at least I know what's wrong.

I'm allergic to milk.

Well that doesn't seem too bad. I mean, no more cold cereal in the morning, no wonder I was always sick, but at least I'll be well.

I start to worry about calcium deficiency. I can probably get some tablets.

And what's more I've found out myself without any help from my wretch of a doctor and now I won't die and he won't get hold of my valuable comics.

The attack begins to subside some hours later and I start to feel pretty good.

Milk? Who needs it?

There were only eighteen issues of the Silver
Surfer. They were good comics. Marvel's best comics always go to the wall due to lack of sales. Where are you now, Howard the Duck? Whatever happened to the Warlock? Killraven? Captain Marvel?

Captain Marvel was a Kree warrior who loved Una, the only main female character in American comics ever to have short hair and not look like a Barbie doll. Una was killed through the evil machinations of the commander of Captain Marvel's spaceship, who loved her as well.

Later on a gruesome space parasite took over Una's body. After viciously attacking Carol Danvers (later to become Ms. Marvel and be given her own series, also to be cancelled) she/it slugs it out with Captain Marvel. The Kree warrior feels bad about fighting Una, even though it is only her body inhabited by this creature. As he wins the battle and life slips away from the space parasite, Una's eyes clear for a second and her true self seems to exist there for an instant. Then she is dead and cold.

The Chinese man has given up his hunt for the day and does not plan to come looking in person again. Tomorrow he will hire someone to find Alby Starvation for him.

Cheng drives him back into town, drops him off, and heads for his favourite video store. He checks carefully that Wu is not around, or anyone else who might recognise him. Being caught buying a game to practise on would be very bad for his credibility. When he is satisfied that the coast is clear he strides into the shop and buys a module of the game that occupies most of his thoughts these days. Kill Another One, it's called.

He hurries home and gets down to some serious practising.

I give sulphate to Fran and Julie and they say thank you and give me some money. They know already about the Chinese man who is looking for me. Everyone knows, they say. What does he want?

I tell them I don't know specifically but it certainly involves harm to my person. You should have seen the vicious looking character who was with him I expect he wants to take over my business you know what these big time gangsters are like remember Paul Muni in "Scarface"?

Fran seems doubtful and shakes her cropped head. "Why would anyone bother trying to take over your trade, Alby? It's pretty small."

"Megalomania?"

I get pissed off that they're casting doubt on the danger I'm in from this oriental demon when I've more or less got scars on my ears where he threw the shuriken at me.

Perhaps he is connected with the killer from the Milk Marketing Board. I consider bombing their premises, serve the bastards right, but I wouldn't know how to go about it. Of course everyone in this country is hoping very much for no more bombs planted anywhere in case there happens to be a horse nearby which gets wounded as the last time this happened this horse was front-page news for the rest of the month with interviews and books and if it happens again then we will probably be subjected to a TV series.

I sit and drink tea with Fran, and Julie absent-mindedly swings kicks at chairs and walls and things and Fran puts on a record but these home comforts cannot keep from my mind the fact that the entire London underworld is hot on my trail.

I ask them if they know how to get hold of a gun but all they give me is pitying looks. I begin to wonder if they are in on the plot. I mean, Fran has never actually expressed open interest in my comics but you never know. You can't trust anyone these days. The last time I went to Big Value the security guard gave me a filthy look.

After I'm cured I naturally tell people and strangely I meet someone who suffers from similar appalling symptoms. She tries out the cure and by coincidence it turns out that she is also allergic to milk. She gets better.

One day I'm walking along when I meet this same person. She tells me that she's met someone else suffering from an illness and getting the brush-off from the medical profession and would I come along and explain how to fast and test for an allergy because she is not sure that she can explain it all properly.

So I do. The person turns out to be highly allergic to milk. He gets better. This third person is called Ian and he is a reporter for a small local paper. He writes a little article and for some reason the editor prints it and the story makes out that this allergy detection technique is mine, which it isn't, it's Stacey's.

From there things seem to snowball somehow. It would still have been all right if it hadn't turned out that so many people were allergic to milk.

I received a tip-off that this killer was after me and that she was working on a contract which had been put out on me. I was lucky to get this tip-off.

But I couldn't flee Brixton completely because the hamster is scared of living anywhere else so I moved and laid low, hoping that by the time I was found I would be in a position to defend myself. I hoped that eventually it might blow over. But then I heard from various sources that a Chinese man was looking for me as well. Is it possible to die from fear and stress? Well if it is I'll be shuffling off pretty soon, my life was fairly simple a little while ago, sick yes, but simple. All of a sudden I'm Britain's most wanted man.

Do we have a list of the most wanted people in Britain? Do they really have one in the USA, or just in the movies?

Here's an idea for a story. The tenth most wanted man in America is annoyed to be only tenth because he thinks he's a pretty mean character and deserves to be higher up the list. So he tracks down number eight and kills him. This act bumps him up into the new number eight spot but number nine is furious to be overtaken like this and goes out hunting for him.

News gets out and into the papers. This gives other people on the list ideas and number three announces that as far as he is concerned he's America's most wanted man and as soon as he can get his hands on number one he's going to prove it.

People start taking bets on the outcome of these battles and the newspapers start publishing the wanted list as a daily league. As the men on the list get killed or captured, vacancies occur and there is such furious rivalry to get on that a second division has to be formed with strict rules for promotion. The police wouldn't mind if the criminals were only killing each other but they have taken to committing horrific crimes against the public in the hope of being promoted up the list and every day civilians are mown down by young hopefuls while the old hands do things like poisoning the water supplies of major cities.

I don't know how the story would end. (The president sends them all off to Central America as policy advisors?)

I like Fran and Julie even though they don't give me anywhere near enough sympathy. Fran asks me if I'm coming to the gig tonight and I say yes, I'll probably be as safe there as anywhere. Julie remarks slyly that she hasn't seen my name in the papers for a while and I give her a big scowl because I'd rather not think about it.

"Why are you always kicking things?" I ask Julie. I know what she's going to reply.

"I'm pretending they're men."

"How can you hate all men when I'm such a wonderful person?" Neither of them answers.

Julie has lots of hair that includes all the main colours and several shades. She learns kung fu in a women-only class in a nearby squat and sometimes she helps to teach the beginners.

I've never done any martial art because I'm too scared of getting hurt.

Fran changes the record. She puts on the Gymslips who are a sort of female punk band well not exactly punk but sort of well fuck it I'm not a music critic she puts on the Gymslips. Reggae is sort of frowned upon in the household because it's often blatantly sexist though this is not an iron rule especially when they are drugged to the eyeballs.

They ask how the hamster is and I tell them he's fine, he's been going out a lot and he's asking for them. Is there some bit of this missed out? I mean, are you clear on everything so far?

Wu, Cheng's deadly rival round the arcades, never practises. Instead he meditates. He is one of the few people to practise the art of zen video gaming. He meditates till his mind is empty and then he becomes one with the machine. When he comes to the realisation that the machine is part of him and he is part of the machine and the temporality of the game is an illusion, then the game just happens. He plays without objective consciousness.

While the foolish might say that video games are not a suitable field in which to practise zen, Wu knows better. It's the same as anything else.

Whilst Cheng is seeking personal glory, Wu seeks spiritual advancement. His oneness with the world of games is such that he can change his perception to that of the machine and play on the person standing outside.

As a result of all his meditation Wu is an exceptionally calm person. Even in arcade skirmishes he exudes quiet and calm. More or less everyone he comes into contact with is impressed by this and most people like him.

Sometimes lonely people stand close to him in the arcade to draw comfort from his positive vibrations.

If he knew that Cheng was practising at home in direct violation of the spirit of their contests he would not mind.

Although he is a good cook he eats very simply and sometimes fasts. Right now he is boiling some rice and then he's going to meditate again.

When I had some money I bought a drum machine. It's good because you can tell it what to do, which is more than I can say for any human drummer I've ever met.

But now that I'm no longer a national hero I'm appallingly hard up. I can't even afford to buy a newspaper and consequently I never really know what day it is or what's happening in the Middle East. I tried watching television but I couldn't take it in. I was pleased when it broke and I didn't have to worry about being arrested by a TV detector van any more. Everyone says they don't work but it would be just typical if one of them miraculously burst into life outside my flat.

Everyone I know is broke, no one ever has any money apart from a brief flurry on giro day, sitting celebrating this fortnight's pittance in the pub and maybe even lashing out and buying something to eat.

Fran is offering me some food, which I appreciate.

"I wish I could shoplift like you," I say to her, "but I'm too scared I'd get caught."

"So what if you did?" says Fran. "It wouldn't be the end of the world, would it?"

"No, but it would be awful embarrassing."

We're eating and this unusual event makes me forget my troubles for a while. The radio is on. A government minister is warning peace protesters that if they get inside a military base they may be shot.

Merton council announces that it is abolishing school dinners.

Two weeks after Ian's local newspaper article two people write simultaneously to the paper saying that they'd cured themselves of lingering diseases by using the method described. They both express their gratitude to me by name.

When four more letters appeared a reporter came down to interview me.

"How did you discover," he asks, "that milk is potentially poisonous?"

I tell him that I really had no idea that it was and only found out by trial and error. The next day they run a story. The headline is ANTI-MILK CAMPAIGNER LASHES OUT.

The reason that June got the elimination job is that she is very discreet. Her employers are very respectable and cannot risk exposure. They have already taken out one contract on the anti-milk campaigner's life with an agency where they have an account but it has been hopelessly bungled, so now they have decided to hire June. Although she commands an enormous fee, her reputation for efficiency and discretion is second to none.

But June has already established that her quarry has gone to ground and can no longer be found at the address her clients have given her. Fortunately she has skills of detection as well as destruction, so she offers to locate the anti-milk campaigner. For this she charges an extra fee, also enormous, but her clients don't want to involve yet another agency in what should have been a straightforward contract and so they agree to her terms.

The situation is slightly confused by the fact that while in the public eye her target has been using a false name. The reason for this, though June does not know it, is that he does not want the social security to stop his giro, which they will do at the slightest excuse if they thought he was receiving any money.

She realises that it may be awkward finding this person now that he appears to have fled into hiding but with the dossier of information she has on him she does not think that it will take too long.

June heads uptown to the comic shop to buy some bait.

She buys some rare expensive early numbers of the *Fantastic Four* and an *Incredible Hulk* No. 1.

Carefully packing them in her bag she heads on home.

The sun shines over Brixton and causes pain to everyone working inside shops hot with people and noisy with cash tills. The assistants behind the tills at Big Value suppress conscious thought, becoming robotic in an effort to defeat the tedium of the work.

Occasionally the chief security guard wanders behind them making salacious comments. He thinks he is a big hit with these girls and that they admire and respect his uniform.

They think he is a wanker and frequently say so.

His uniform is blue with white trimmings. Around the shelves other security people skulk. They are plain-clothed store detectives and they act suspiciously, following people they don't like the look of. They like to pretend that they can spot a thief by intuition but what they generally do is follow people who look poor. Regular visitors to the shop know them by sight and young people often point them out to each other.

"Her over there with the brown coat," or "that man who's been watching us for the last ten minutes."

Nobody is watched as carefully as the employees themselves.

I'm walking home up the hill. I look compulsively in shop windows to see what I look like. This depresses me. I wish I had a paper bag to put over my head.

When I get in I talk to the hamster and this cheers me up a bit. He tells me what he's been up to and I tell him my problems. He is sympathetic but not really in a position to help. We talk about reggae and dancing.

If I'm reincarnated I'd like to come back as a hamster, in fact I think I was meant to be one this time round and this accidental occupation of a human shell is the root of my problems. There's no way of appealing against your current incarnation however, so I leave the hamster to go back to sleep and wander through to the kitchen to examine the cupboards.

In a sudden fit of optimism I decide to make an apple crumble and give the kitchen table a desultory wipe in preparation. Then I pile the ingredients up and scout around for a mixing bowl. As always I cannot remember the correct proportions and anyway I don't possess any scales so I just throw approximate amounts of flour and margarine into a bowl and mash them round for a while. When it seems too wet I put in more flour and then I have to put in more margarine to compensate and eventually I end up with a giant bowlful of crumble mixture and hardly any room to cram in the sugar. There is about four times as much mixture as would fit in my only cooking dish.

Meanwhile the apples are simmering away in a pot and the oven is heating up. The thermostat on the oven has broken and the heat doesn't cut off at any set temperature, it just keeps on getting hotter. Consequently it's like cooking in a furnace and only possible due to my highly developed intuition honed over years of dealing with worn-out kitchen equipment.

But it comes out quite well so I give a bit to the hamster and sit down to eat the rest. This small success gives me deep satisfaction.

And then I have nothing to do all day but wait around till it's time for Fran's gig and worry in case any of my enemies suddenly burst through the door waving machetes or handguns. Perhaps I could transport my comics uptown on the bus in a suitcase? I estimate that this would involve about twelve trips and take several days.

Someone knocks on the door and I freeze in panic.

I hate people knocking on the door at the best of times and this is not the best of times. Deep in my subconscious a prayer starts to tick over just in case the still widely held belief in God should have any foundation in truth.

The knock comes again. I get down flat and worm my way along the hall and then flow like a snake up the door to the peephole. Outside it's my friend Stacey. Unless he's sold me out and is enticing me to open the door prior to being riddled with bullets, I'm safe for the moment.

Stacey comes in and tells me he's just met a woman down the second-hand bookshop in Brixton who was asking if anyone knew where she could sell some valuable comics she had. He tells me that he told her he knew someone who would be interested and gave her my phone number.

I start to cry.

Cheng is practising like crazy at Kill Another One. He is becoming lethally skilled at it, sitting in front of his television at home with the game module plugged in and the lights off, *zap zap zap*.

He chain smokes though most of the time his hands are too busy to get the cigarette to his mouth and long tubes of ash crumble onto the carpet. When the game ends he takes a draw from the short stub that remains and lights another. As his concentration intensifies he starts to sweat and his brow solidifies into a thick ridge of lines but his wrists and fingers stay soft and supple.

You bastard Wu, he thinks. I'll fix you this time.

It's hard to explain to Stacey why I am crying. In between sniffles I give him a rough outline of my predicament and impress on him that in all probability he has given my phone number to someone who is going to kill me. He asks me why I don't flee the country immediately and I begin to see that he too is after my comics, soon as I'm gone he is jemmying down my front door and loading up with early editions of *Conan*.

I try to get rid of him. Before I throw him out I get him to give me a cigarette.

Well, the next stage in my rise to fame is I'm interviewed by an independent radio station and after their news report a magazine phones me up for an interview wanting to know my tips on nutrition and how to avoid illness.

All of a sudden half the country seems to be suffering from hidden allergies, most of them allergies to milk.

The Milk Marketing Board reacts quickly and puts it down to lies and mass hysteria but the nation is not convinced. I appear on television to tell my story and people start sending donations to help in the campaign, as they now call it.

Well up until now the whole thing had seemed like a complete pain and why won't these people leave me alone I don't know anything about medicine or nutrition, but when people send money I begin to see things in a new light.

On television I castigate the milk authorities for covering up the facts.

Around this time the Milk Marketing Board
is running a campaign around the slogan "Milk's Gotta Lotta Bottle."

This is an insult to the intelligence and really you think that anyone thinking up such a slogan would hide the fact immediately, but no, they're going hard at it, implying in the campaign that milk is no drink for softies and just the thing you want if you're a cowboy or a mountaineer. They are sponsoring football competitions and getting their product sold in pubs and generally covering the entire country in advertising posters promoting the new macho milk image.

Alarm bells start ringing at Milk Headquarters when news of the adverse publicity gets out. Their April sales figures are not as high as expected, though it is too soon to tell if this is due to the bad publicity or some other national phenomenon like people being too poor to buy cornflakes any more.

Matters are brought to the attention of the dirty tricks department at Milk Headquarters. This department is modelled on the similarly named part of the CIA and liaises closely with the sales and publicity departments.

Their job is to rubbish any opposition to milk. Anyone that comes out with anything that might be harmful to their sales is subject to a campaign of lies, threats, and disinformation till the danger they pose is nullified.

They are headed by a ruthless ex-salesman called Crosby. His second in command is an ex-government psychologist named Withers. As things start to look bad they swing into action. Crosby sends Withers out to get the dirt on the new diet nut who is troubling them and Withers gets to work with his team of spies and computer technicians.

June is generally not too fond of people and does not mind that her work tends to reduce their number. In her whole life she has only met three people who she even vaguely liked.

She doesn't dislike people on principle. It's just that she doesn't like the things they say or do.

She never has sex, though she would quite like to, because she would only sleep with someone she liked. She doesn't even have conversations very often and she lives alone in a flat in Chelsea surrounded by plants and philosophy books. The plants live in pots of all different sizes, including one enormous trench-like furrow in the living room that contains some of her larger favourites. Much of the wall and floor space is covered in vegetation. It's not that she's absolutely crazy about plants, just that she doesn't like most man-made decorations.

Her collection of philosophy books is vast and well read. Some time ago she came to the conclusion that almost all of the philosophy contained in the books had nothing to offer her, which saddened her somewhat as any clue to the purpose of living would have been very welcome.

She has also gone off the philosophy books because she suddenly realised that the authors were all men. Not unreasonably, she decided that this would colour their world view and lessen their value to her.

When she kills someone she doesn't feel as if she has committed a real act, like buying coffee at a supermarket or jumping off a bus at the traffic lights. After it's over she doesn't feel like she's done anything at all.

Although she does not keep any records, she reckons that she has performed about fourteen assassinations. Her booking agent provides her with a new one more or less any time she needs the money. Sometimes he gets in touch with her and says he's got an urgent job and will she do it. Sometimes she will and sometimes she won't.

In his little house the hamster turns over contentedly and drifts back to sleep.

He is specially adapted by nature to sleep comfortably in all positions.

During the day all he does is eat and sleep.

He could do a lot more but he doesn't see much point.

Wu has just finished meditating.

He smiles and looks around him. He lives in one room and it is completely bare. The only thing in it is a futon. He shares a kitchen with some other people downstairs. There is no clock in the room because Wu generally knows what time it is and anyway he doesn't mind. There is no chair because he always sits on a cushion on the floor. There is only a plain wooden box in which he keeps his painting materials.

Sometimes Wu paints. He practises Zen painting and makes designs that mean more to him than to other people. He paints moving space. Some of his paintings are intrinsically beautiful and anyone seeing them is usually impressed. Wu does not exhibit his paintings but he does not mind people seeing them. Sometimes somebody wants to buy one and Wu is happy to sell it to them cheaply.

There is a big noise outside my flat. For one shuddering moment I think it's a rocket being launched, Jesus, who have they hired to get me, the SAS?

But it turns out to be a workman digging up the road. I study him for a time but he seems harmless enough so I get back to worrying about what to do when this killer phones me up, why the fuck can't she have a heart attack and leave me in peace, look, did I start any of this?

Maybe I could disguise my voice to sound like a doctor from Wales or somewhere and answer the phone pretending to have officiated at a quick death, he passed away quietly ten minutes ago, his heart wasn't what it was, it just wouldn't carry him up all these stairs any more. We pleaded with the council for years to give him a ground floor flat. Or I could be an undertaker saying is that the flower shop send round a few more cheap wreaths we've discovered he had some friends after all, funny isn't it, the house is full of them, all rummaging through his comic collection.

Outside the man is having a hard time digging up the road. He is all by himself without even a Youth Opportunities Person to help him and by the time he has erected warning lights and fences and his little tent-like contraption to sit in when the rain comes down, he is exhausted. Now he is wrestling with a drilling machine he can't control very well and seems in constant danger of cutting off his foot.

The reason that he is on his own is that he is not really a council road digger at all but an imposter. Over the past few months he has meticulously stolen everything he needs to set up his own roadworks, a flashing light from here, a donkey jacket from there, every night walking the streets in search of more equipment to make his site realistic. His final act, stealing the drill, involved burgling the works department and dragging weighty equipment into a council van, a van he had previously stolen by connecting the wires in a technique he learned from an American cop programme he had been watching specially to pick up criminal hints, and driving coolly out into the night. He had spent some weeks disguising the van so that it still looked like it belonged to the council, but could not be identified as the stolen vehicle.

The reason behind all this criminal activity is that Professor Wing, as he is called, has discovered, through extensive study of documents in the British Library, that an ancient crown, last seen at the time of King Ethelred the Unready, is buried at this precise spot. Professor Wing does not intend for anyone else to get their hands on it before he does. Although his physique is not well-suited to digging holes in the road he is prepared to suffer in the cause of knowledge.

His shrewd appraisal of human nature is that once he gets his roadworks set up then no one will trouble him, no matter how incompetent he looks.

Mass hysteria grips the country.

No one who has been sick in the last five years dares to drink milk in case they relapse. There are tales in the papers of terminal cases happily discharging themselves from hospital to begin a new life of health through milklessness. Parents gather outside dairies to burn empty cartons with banners saying STOP POISONING OUR CHILDREN.

I am being interviewed more and more.

The Milk Marketing Board record their worst ever May sales figures.

Money starts to roll in and all the time I'm up at the comic shops and conventions stocking up with valuable comics, or else hanging round reggae shacks being uncool by spending too much money buying too many records. When I get home I listen to the records while entering the comics lovingly in my catalogue, emerging in public only to attend meetings and record interviews.

A publisher gets in touch asking if I'd like to put my name to a ghosted book on eating for health with the possibility of also putting my name to a new partwork, get issue two free with issue one. *The Starvation Guide to Healthy Eating*? It just doesn't sound right. Why do people buy these crummy partworks anyway? Do they ever get beyond a few issues, does anyone want a roomful of glossy needlework tips?

A newspaper asks me if I'd like to send a message on nutrition to our boys serving in far-off parts of the world.

To take my mind off my troubles I get to work programming a murderous new rhythm into my drum machine. I get the beat in my head and write it down in a notation I made up myself on the back of an old gas bill envelope, then tap it out on the programming buttons. The drum machine connects to the amplifier in my bedroom. I set the switch to play and when it comes on it turns out just right, just how I wanted it. I turn it up loud and it pounds through the flat. I'm dancing away happily to my new rhythm when the phone rings and I answer it without thinking.

A female voice that I don't recognise asks for me by name and I know that this is the killer but I don't hang up because it has dawned on me that the only way of freeing myself from this threat is by militantly annihilating it.

She introduces herself as Pamela Patterson and says she's got some valuable comics to get rid of and someone in Brixton told her I might be interested.

I'm acting natural as best I can, voice to voice with someone who is planning to remove me from the face of the earth, and I tell her that yes I may well be interested and she says how about if I come and see you, where do you live?

"Well, that would be a bit inconvenient just now," I tell her, sitting down as my knees give way. "Why don't we meet somewhere?"

"How about tomorrow?" she says.

"How about next week?" I shout over the noise of the drum machine.

She says no, she really would like to see me sooner. Thinking like lightning I realise that if I try and stall her too much then she will track me down to my flat and kill me here.

"Monday?" I suggest. She agrees. I got two days to make a plan.

At least I don't have to worry tonight. I go and put my head in the speaker.

While Withers is out researching the hopefully
murky past of their target, Crosby, the head of the dirty tricks
department, is called to a meeting of top milk executives. The May sales
figures have just come in and everyone is in deep gloom interrupted
only by spasms of rage and fear.

Sales figures have plummeted and the Milk's Gotta Lotta Bottle
campaign is in ruins.

"There is no time," Crosby is told, "to do a complicated disinformation job. Get rid of him."

"Right you are," says Crosby.

I've beaten myself into submission with the drum machine and I'm
recovering on the radio.

An advert comes on for Leeds Castle in Sussex (Is Leeds in Sussex?
My English geography is not too hot but I feel that it is not), as well as
being the most beautiful castle in the world this establishment boasts
the world's only dog collar museum.

This is stunning news. A dog collar museum. How many kinds of dog collars are there? Do they come in hundreds of different varieties? Is the place full of historically significant dog collars, this one was worn by the Tsar's poodle in 1917 and was smuggled out of the USSR by a loyal White Russian general, this one was worn by Bessie the first dog to orbit the earth, this one was found among the ruins of Pompeii, this one was worn by one of the Sex Pistols?

I take a mental note to tell everyone I know about it, and if any interesting dog collars come into my possession then I will certainly be sending them off straight away.

I spend hours getting ready to go out. No one else could notice at the end of it all that I look any different to when I started out but every little thing is vitally important to me. I'm staring in the mirror for about an hour solid, depressed about the way I look. How did I get to be so old?

Is it possible to go backwards? Will facemarks ever come into fashion? Why don't I look better? The streets are packed full of pretty people with young faces and good complexions. How come I look like a radiation-mutant?

Deep down I'm convinced that I look pretty good but people conspire against me to hide it. Bastards. Leave me alone.

I drag out the entire contents of my wardrobe, well cupboard, and try everything on with everything else. On the radio the Norwegians are hunting for a suspected Soviet submarine in the waters round their coast. This seems to be happening all the time these days though why I have no idea.

Then I start from the beginning and try everything on with everything else again and get pretty mad because nothing looks right and why the fuck don't I have any good clothes though even if I had I don't suppose it would make much difference and they will probably refuse me entrance to the gig tonight even though the place where it is being held is an utter dive with rats and beer glasses swilling round the floor.

I sit down and sniff some speed for encouragement.

Eventually I find some ragged destroyed garments that hang on me in a fairly satisfactory manner, they come from several of my favourite junk shops and resemble hand-me-downs from a large Victorian family. Suitably dressed at last I wander despairingly round every room in the flat looking for everything I need to stuff into my pockets to go out with. I can't find my keys and have reached the stage of lifting the furniture to check underneath when I accidentally stumble across them behind one of these plastic squeezy things you water plants with and then I seem to be ready.

"Goodbye Happy," I say to the hamster. "Have a nice time if you decide to go out."

I check in the shadows for killers. I can't find any so I hurry down the hill. The wind blows my hair around and I curse it.

The wind is always blowing on me and I think there is something personal in it.

Professor Wing has packed up for the day. He is satisfied to have started but slightly worried in case his calculations are wrong. If they are even slightly out then he is in trouble. Digging up the road in Brixton is not like digging in the desert somewhere, you can't just move over a few yards for another try if the first one fails, not when it's just you and a stolen drill you can't.

He spends the evening examining manuscripts that he has removed illegally from the British Library. He will put them back when he no longer needs them. After he gets the crown anyone is welcome to use them but right now he figures that his need is greatest.

The crown was famous in Ethelred's time. It is reputed to have great magical powers and was stolen by an evil magician who wanted to use it in his continuing war against some do-gooder in the neighbouring county.

Big Value is quiet now. The only person in the shop, alone in the semi-darkness of his office, is the manager. Gloom pours out of the ceiling and travels through his head down his spine right into his smart shoes.

He is depressed about the sales figures and also the figures for stolen goods, goods misappropriated, as far as he is concerned, by his thieving staff in collusion with the shoplifters who wander unhampered through the aisles of his store.

He imagines some pre-arranged meeting place in Brixton, the security guards and cash-till assistants getting together with the vast posses of shoplifters to share out the day's proceeds.

He is particularly depressed because the poor figures mean that he won't get the bonus he was hoping for and that means he won't be able to buy a Swedish-style Pinelog Chalet Pool. He reads their advertisement.

Who says you can't buy health and happiness? With a Pinelog Chalet Pool you can enjoy exhilarating relaxation, soothe away muscular aches and pains, celebrate a return to good health, and have fun into the bargain.

Wallow in hydrotherapeutic splendour and be lulled into well-being by the powerful jets of the spa, or, without going to great lengths, practise your swimming on the spot against the optional Swinijet Module.

As for size, with a pool-length of only eighteen feet, you won't have to bulldoze the rockery to accommodate the chalet in your garden, and it can be tailor-made to any configuration you name. Optional extras include sauna, solarium, bar, shower, and toilet.

A complete installation can cost just £15,000, normally without the need for planning consent. For more information and a copy of our illustrated brochure, fill in the coupon and send to Pinelog Products Ltd.

For some time the manager has been wishing that he was more fit but he never seems to have time to exercise or be able to cut down on smoking and drinking. Getting fit by lying round in an eighteen-foot pool seems like a more practical idea.

Cheng and Wu and many others are heading for the Golden Glitter Arcade for tonight's round of their continuing battle. The owner of the arcade is pleased when they come because they bring trade with them, both for the machines he runs and the rent boys he pimps for.

The rent boys are young male prostitutes who hang around the arcade. The owner takes a high proportion of their earnings. As well as their contributions to the owner, the boys have to pay money to the police to avoid being arrested too often. The police also take a cut from the money the boys give to the owner in addition to their normal rake-off from his arcade. This does not leave the boys with very much but they have nowhere else to go and no other way of getting money. Most of them are young runaways from Scotland and the north of England. They are scared of the owner and scared of being sent home. The owner is a crook with unpleasant associates. The last time one of the boys ran away the police arrested him for soliciting and locked him up for a few days to teach him a lesson. Then they handed him back to the arcade.

Cheng and Wu are aware that the arcade is not a very nice place but they are not aware of the virtual slavery of the boys.

When the people playing Kill Another One see Cheng and Wu coming in they immediately stop playing, even if they have only just put their money into the machine. This is partly out of respect and partly because it would be too embarrassing for anyone else to play Kill Another One in front of Wu and Cheng.

People shout encouragement to whichever player they support and cluster tightly around the machines. The contestants exchange greetings. Cheng's is blatantly insincere and even Wu finds it hard to be enthusiastic in greeting someone who so obviously hates him.

They used to be friends.

Hiring a killer was no trouble for Withers.

His department has an account with an agency which deals with such things and though they have never actually had anyone killed up till now they have done such damage to several people as to cause them to commit suicide. Crosby and Withers have personally harmed hundreds of people during their careers.

The agency takes the contract and contacts one of their gunmen, a person by the name of Alton. They pay him a deposit and he goes off on his mission.

But on his way through Brixton he gets handed a leaflet by a middle-aged woman. The leaflet asks "Has Jesus come into your life?" and before he can throw it away be gets a blinding flash inside his head. A mighty voice seems to speak to him.

He looks down at the leaflet. It reads:

> Do you know that two thousand years ago a man was born in Jerusalem called Jesus Christ?
> He never held office.
> He never went to school.
> He never got a degree.
> He was born a humble carpenter.
> He never travelled more than fifty miles from his birth place.
> He never left the country.
> He was crucified with criminals.
> Yet today this man, the son of God, is the most important figure in the history of the world. Do you know him?
> For more information contact the World Movement for Christianity, c/o the World Movement for Freedom.

The inherent power contained in the leaflet's words have a profound effect on Alton and he is immediately converted. Deeply sorry for all his past crimes he rushes to the home of his intended victim to warn him of the danger he is in. Then he rushes back to Brixton to help hand out leaflets.

In the middle of my fame and popularity I'm visited by this utter madman who stands ranting and prophesying on my doorstep for perhaps ten minutes before coming to the point.

"Do you know Jesus?" he bawls at me.

"Well, not personally."

He gives me the big eye. "Well you might not have much time left."

"Whaddya mean?"

He rants for a while more about the Book of Revelations and abortions and various other things and I finally get the idea that he is warning me personally rather than just the world in general.

He tells me that there's a contract out on my life. I presume that this is some church attempt at hipspeak and means the devil's after my soul or something and I'm on the point of closing the door, should never have opened it in the first place, the only people who call on me are meter readers and lunatics.

But I'm just shutting the door when I hear the words "Milk Marketing Board."

I'm thoughtful for a while. I look at the leaflet he forced on me. I never knew Jesus was born in Jerusalem.

Outside a voice sings "Jesu joy of man's desiring." I wonder who Jesu is, but don't open the door again to ask.

The Chinese man, Cheng's employer, is hanging round an expensive nightclub without enjoying himself very much. The place is full of middle-aged men in suits and young men in suits who seem to be middle-aged anyway and most of them are slightly drunk and getting noisier and noisier as the evening goes on and dancing in such a fashion as would deeply embarrass anyone but the drunken rich.

In amongst them and hanging round there are girls. Some of them are rich and go to the club because they are only happy socialising with their own kind, but many of them are far from rich and it is blatantly obvious that these women are only there and only speak to the men because they have lots of money. The men don't seem to mind, having a girl's attention makes them feel good, it's not as if they are prostitutes after all, that would make them feel not so good.

The Chinese man owns a part share in the club and consequently has to put in personal appearances now and then. A man who is a lord slaps him on the back as he passes. Cheng watches and smiles and thinks what a hopeless specimen he is.

"You are enjoying yourself, Lord Wainwright?"

"Rather!" Lord Wainwright stumbles off.

Most people in Britain don't say "rather" any more.

So then this madman appeared on my doorstep singing about Jesu and telling me that the Milk Marketing Board have put a contract out on my life.

It's ridiculous, I mean they're meant to be a responsible body. They're funded by the public, it's my taxes that keep them in business. Well it would be if I had a job. Or are they funded by the public? Now I think about it I'm not sure. But anyway, they can't go around just killing anyone they take a dislike to.

This puts a new light on the mysterious death last summer of that much-loved TV celebrity who was making such a hit with all those beer commercials.

Immediately I'm frantic with worry and start avoiding the windows in my flat, I've seen these people on television focussing their telescopic sights from neighbouring tower blocks, bastards, screwing the sights and other complicated bits of equipment onto their sniper's rifles with hands that are covered by thin black leather gloves, these killers got rich faces, they never look old before their time like us that suffer, it's probably one of the cushiest jobs you can get, just shooting the odd person in between lying around on a yacht or holidaying in some expensive resort.

One consolation of poverty is the appalling lack of taste exhibited by those who are in possession of money, their flabby bodies hiding in expensive clothes, hanging around fantastically expensive places like a bunch of tailors' dummies.

Someone's gonna shoot me.

At his house Professor Wing is sitting at an enormous table over which are spilled maps, books, and manuscripts. In amongst these documents are his own papers. Pens and pencils roll regularly onto the floor. Underneath the table there are some working man's tools that have no regular place of abode in the professor's house.

He is checking his calculations for the hundredth time. He appreciates that it's a bit late to find out that they are wrong now that he's begun digging up the pavement but on the other hand he is too sensible to carry on if he finds out he has made some error.

He got the first clue as to the existence of the crown in a manuscript in the British Library. This manuscript gave no hint as to its whereabouts however, and the break-through didn't come until he found an ancient sheet of parchment inside a 1959 *Beano* annual that he was buying for a colleague of his who collected them.

He happened to know that his colleague had a complete collection of *Beano* annuals apart from 1948 and 1959 and when he came across it in a junk shop, which he was perusing for no particular reason, he bought it immediately, pleased to do him a favour.

When he gets the annual home he naturally wants to read it before handing it over. Inside he finds the ancient piece of parchment. It is couched in obscure language but after only a quick look Professor Wing realises it has something to do with the crown he has recently been reading about. He trembles with excitement and thinks no more of the incongruity of finding such a document in an old *Beano* annual.

The document is hundreds and hundreds of years old but has lain for most of the time in the bottom drawer of a cabinet which was made in the year 800. The cabinet was buried when the castle in which it stood suffered destruction in one of Britain's rare earthquakes.

Thus protected it is unearthed many centuries later by a company excavating a field for a new sewage system. Although they call in experts when they start finding antique furniture and bits of castle, the parchment flutters away by accident without anyone noticing.

It lands beside one of the workmen and he gathers it up accidentally with the paper that his sandwiches were wrapped up in and takes it home in his lunch box.

He finds it later but mistakes it for a letter from his lover so he hides it quickly under the couch where one of his children finds it and after folding it into the shape of a glider and flying it around for a while she puts it to use as a bookmark.

Which is why it turned up inside the *Beano* annual.

All this talk of hired killers worries me a bit at the time, though when I think about it rationally my fears diminish a little, I mean, surely the Milk Marketing Board isn't really going to hire someone to kill me? How could they hide the expense on their tax returns?

Maybe they wouldn't have to hide it. It might be a legitimate business practice under the Conservatives. They might even offer incentives.

And that man had sounded quite convincing, and his pocket had bulged with what could have been a weapon. Still, religious fanatics are notorious cranks and probably he made the whole thing up in an effort to sell me a book or something.

I'm trying to do some push-ups. It's too hard, my arms hurt and bend, how do people ever manage to pick up those gigantic weights?

Perhaps the television coverage of weightlifting competitions is carefully faked in order to generate a feeling of inferiority among the population as a whole. Every day I see wretches in shorts trotting round my housing estate in expensive running shoes and I really get mad because I couldn't run more than twelve yards in an emergency and I hate to see people do something I can't do. I plan alternately to get myself fit or harass the joggers.

I'm just trying to think where my watch might be when someone knocks on the door, I always hate unexpected knocks on the door, when did it ever bring me anything good, perhaps you could all consider just leaving me alone for a while?

I grumble and answer it to a little man who is on first glance an obvious maniac escaped from a psychiatric establishment. He flashes a card at me and it says John Primrose.

"I'm from the Milk Marketing Board," he says.

I go faint and wait for the bullet to strike.

"They'd kill me if they knew I'd come here," he continues, "but I wanted to help you because your campaign cured my son. He'd been ill all his life and we'd had him looked at by doctors from six countries. Now he just misses out on milk and a few other things and he's the healthiest person in the street—" I interrupt the testimonial to ask him why he has come.

"They're going to hire a new killer," he says, "a woman, trained by the Brazilian secret police. They think she won't be so easily distracted as the last one. Thanks for saving my son." He rushes off.

That was the time when I decided to move.

Divers are staging a sit-in on the floor of the North Sea in a dispute over pay and conditions.

This is certainly an impressive way to protest, I think, won't they die if they hang around on the seabed? It seems brave to the point of foolishness to go down there in the first place, can it be worth staying there for any reason? I imagine the sea is packed full of sharks and squids and poisonous seaweed not to mention hostile submarines and deep sea pirates with harpoon guns and all in all it's not a place that I have a great urge to visit.

The manager of Big Value finally goes home. His wife is worried about him because he has not bothered to phone home and tell her where he is or that he is going to be late. He is sorry about this now because he likes his wife. But he is always so worried by his troubles at work that he never seems able to act nicely or even thoughtfully and this saddens his wife because she likes him as well.

"These bastards are robbing me blind," he says in reply to his wife's greeting.

She wonders what they can eat. The food she prepared for their evening meal is blackened and dead in the oven. She doesn't mention it for fear of upsetting him more.

"I wish that bastard Wilkins would die." Wilkins is the area manager and they both see him as responsible for not promoting him to a better Big Value.

The manager's wife would like a new cat to keep her company during the day because she has a lonely life and her only contact with the world is when she is out shopping and even then it is only for minor things because her husband brings home most of the food they need from the store. But she can't bring up the subject of a cat because of what happened to the last one and the smear it put on her husband.

Her husband has been wondering if the cat really had cancer of the throat or if the vet might not have been in league with Wilkins and given a false diagnosis to discredit him. The vet was a shifty character and probably only practiced on animals because the Medical Council wouldn't let him near humans. He would not be at all surprised if Wilkins had bribed him.

Just before I get to the blighted little hall where
the gig is to be held, a room underneath a railway arch several yards
square into which people squash their thin unemployed bodies on
Friday and Saturday nights to hear what trash bands there are around,
I meet my friend Jock.

Jock lives with his friend, Sanny, quite close to where I live, and
they both come from Glasgow.

Jock is limping. I know why he is limping, it is because he cut
his leg extremely badly a few months ago when he kicked in a shop
window in a drunken depression. The police arrive and follow the trail
of blood round the corner which naturally leads them to Jock who is
standing in a phone booth with a massive hole in his leg, calling an
ambulance.

They start to question him even though there isn't much to say
about the actual crime. When the ambulance arrives they don't let him
go off in it right away, but keep on questioning him. Jock takes revenge
by bleeding in their car. Eventually they allow the ambulance to take

him to hospital where a doctor sews up his leg with as much care and attention as would be given to a torn mail bag.

While the doctor offhandedly sews up this drunk's leg, the police keep questioning him. Despite the shock and loss of blood, Jock gets no drugs, plasma, or treatment of any kind. The wound leaks blood for several days and feeling never properly returns.

Back in the police station Jock is questioned some more. When he gets up to go to the toilet he gets dizzy and collapses. A police doctor arrives and tells the police that he can't stay in the cells for the night as they intended, he has to go home.

Three days before this happened, Jock's flatmate Sanny was stabbed by the third person who lived in the flat. Sanny was disadvantaged by being in bed at the time. The knife went in his left side and pricked his lung. He gets stitched up at the hospital but he doesn't say who did it to him and Jock pretends he was attacked in the street by a stranger. For a while after this Sanny cannot bend down and Jock cannot reach up so they have to go round their flat together to get things from the shelves and cupboards.

In front of the machines Wu is calm and Cheng is frantic with excitement.

Cheng is winning.

They play on separate machines. They could share one but that would mean constantly changing positions which would waste time. Cheng is piling on points and Wu cannot keep up.

Wu goes deeper and deeper into a meditative trance seeking to merge with the machine in front of him, but for the moment he just cannot match the dazzling display of technique being shown by Cheng.

Cheng has practised his way into grandmastership at Kill Another One and is probably the best player in the world at this moment. Inexorably he pulls further and further ahead of Wu. Those watching, normally amazed by both players' skill, are utterly awed by the way

Cheng is playing and burst into spontaneous applause at each new triumph.

They play for ten minutes at a time, each ten-minute period counts as one game, they fix the number of games they are going to play at the start of the session.

Cheng, slightly behind in the overall series, is winning tonight by six games to nil. Word is spreading and more and more spectators are flocking into the arcade to watch.

Wu is not troubled by the fact that he is losing but he is beginning to have slight doubts of a spiritual nature, thinking that maybe he's not been meditating enough. He tries to ignore such thoughts but finds that he has lost his concentration and cannot empty his mind. He is massacred in the next game.

The gig is black and grimy and quite a lot of fun. I meet Julie in the audience and Fran for a while before she goes off to prepare herself. Her band is on first because they are even more obscure than the other unknown band who top the bill.

When I first get in I look around for any troublemakers who look like they might harass me. It looks relatively safe. I'm due to get killed by a proper killer so there's no point getting knifed by some amateur.

Fran's band thrash out their songs sounding more or less like they only wrote them yesterday. No one dances—well no one does at this sort of thing—but on the other hand no one offers abuse and all things considered the gig goes quite well. No fights start, at least not when Fran's band is on.

Everyone buys the drink they sell illegally in the corner. The band starts another song. It goes *thrash thrash thrash*. They forget a bit in the middle.

"That was the dub version," says Fran from the stage. "We'll play it straight now."

And so they shamble on and finish some time later then wander off stage then wander back almost immediately for an encore and though no one has really asked them to, nobody minds too much.

The song ends and after a while Fran reappears alongside Julie and me. There is an attempt to play some music in between bands but it coughs and splutters into failure before suddenly amplifying into a monstrous crunching noise that sends everybody's hands flying up to cover their pain-wracked ears. After a few seconds of this there is a small electric sigh and the music stops. No one minds.

June the hitperson is listening to the radio. She is bored. She often is bored because there are not many things that she likes to do and more or less no one with whom she likes to do them.

When she can no longer find a programme that she can even tolerate she switches off the radio and puts on her coat. She crams some money into a pocket and leaves the house without thinking where she is going.

She lives in Chelsea, which is expensive, but she can afford it and she appreciates the quietness of her small road. It is cold outside so when she reaches the main road she looks round for a bus and gets on the first one that comes, something that she has done before when life seemed particularly tedious. She doesn't know where the bus is going but pays the maximum fare and just sits for a while upstairs at the front.

After a while she recognises where she is. The bus has taken her to Brixton. She is going to stay on and see what comes next but the lights flash inside and the conductor shouts for everybody to get off. This is as far as the bus is going.

She doesn't really want to get off here because she knows this is where the anti-milk campaigner she is going to kill used to live, and her instincts tell her he hasn't moved far. It doesn't seem like good professional conduct to be wandering round an area where she might accidentally bump into her target, but June is feeling fairly fed up with everything anyway and does not suppose that it will make any difference. Might as well walk these streets for a while, they are as good as any other when you've nothing to do.

So she walks around for a while and looks at the ritzy cinema and the closed and empty market. After a short time she hears music and although the night is turning colder she doesn't feel like going home and being alone she follows it to its source and goes inside. June doesn't like to be lonely but what can you do if the entire world is made up of utter morons?

She pays at the door and squeezes into the gig. Glass crunches under her feet. On stage there is a band made up of four women who seem to be hitting their instruments in a fairly random manner.

She moves over to a space and leans against the wall to look around her.

In the arcade the game has come to an end. Cheng has utterly defeated Wu, his victory is the most conclusive that either of them has ever recorded and his supporters are standing round him with much happy talk and congratulations.

Wu is surprised to have been so heavily defeated and though the loud crowing from the opposite camp does not depress him, it has a bad effect on his followers. They are very upset. Many lonely people who spend their time aimlessly hanging round Soho count themselves as his friends, drawing comfort from his calm aura. They feel the defeat far more than Wu does and he is sorry for them. He knows it is silly for them to feel so involved in what is only a game of no importance, but he also knows that their involvement stems from their regard for him. For reasons he does not fully comprehend these people who support him now seem to need his success and for all his personal contentment he does not know what to say to make any of them feel better.

As they drift off to hang around other arcades or find clients, he starts to walk home. Cheng shouts out a farewell. He sounds malicious and he is. Their rivalry has affected his mind to the point where he can never again be friendly with Wu even if he wins every game they ever play from now on.

"Same time tomorrow, Wu?"

Wu turns and smiles and nods. Then he walks home.

I'm standing round at the gig talking to Fran and Julie then they go off and talk to someone else.

I look around aimlessly and feel slightly foolish because I'm standing in the middle of the floor on my own. Well the place is packed with people and no one could tell I'm on my own but it feels that way anyway so I try and make it to the wall where I can lean with comfort and security, being on your own never seems so bad if there is a wall to lean against. I find a space opposite the bar, that is if two boxes beside each other count as a bar, and strain my neck trying inconspicuously to examine my reflection in the glass. It's quite dark which helps my case but only a little and really I think I look pretty terrible, the strain of being a wanted man on top of the effects of all the illness I had has completely mangled my appearance. Even though for a while I have been more healthy the milk disease has left my skin an unpleasant colour and the terrible suffering I've been through has completely ruined my young looks. It wasn't getting old that did it, it was the sickness.

As I keep straining to examine myself I spill my drink over the person standing next to me.

June is standing at the gig feeling not too bad. She has never been to anything like this before. Being a woman on her own she has to fend off frequent stares and the occasional approach and she does this by concentrating her thoughts on the bodies of the two men she shot in the USA and projecting the image at anyone who looks hopefully at her. It seems to work. And as in an emergency she could beat up anyone who troubled her, she is not too worried.

Someone is standing next to her at the wall but he does not trouble her, possibly because he is too busy looking at his own reflection to notice her. But for no apparent reason other than stupidity he suddenly spills his drink over her.

June is annoyed to have lager running down her leg.

"You cretin," she says. "What did you do that for?"

He seems pathetically sorry, in fact he seems to cringe away from her and his funny-coloured skin pales and he apologises profusely and offers to buy her another drink before remembering that it was his own he spilled.

"An idiot," she thinks.

The Chinese man goes to bed bored and thinks about his business and how well it is going and what troubles lie ahead in the way of rivals and such like. Tomorrow he is going to get in touch with an acquaintance of his who runs a detective agency and hire him to find Alby Starvation.

His mind wanders off the subject of business and on to his personal life. As far as he can see his personal life is non-existent. Somehow his work does not bring him into contact with the sort of girl he would like to meet and this has been troubling him recently. He would like to settle down with a nice young woman from a good family. He would like to start a good family of his own. He appreciates that his line of work might prove to be a problem with her parents but he supposes he could get around that somehow.

He meets girls from affluent families at the club he part owns but he doesn't want to marry anyone who hangs around nightclubs.

He considers placing an advert in a magazine but this is problematic in the extreme as well as being deeply hurtful to his self-esteem. Every week he scans the lonely hearts column of several publications to see if the woman of his dreams might be there in print but she never is. Anyway, he does not know if he would like to meet anyone who advertised themselves in a magazine. And he feels that the sort of woman he would like to meet would not be the sort of person who would reply to an ad either.

So he abandons the idea for the meantime and considers broadening his interests in an effort to widen his social circle. His large-scale drug dealing seems to be something of a barrier however and would necessitate him lying about his background. The problem goes round and round in his head and no solution presents itself and he goes to sleep unhappy.

Fran and Julie, their part in the night's proceeding over, get down to the business of getting wrecked. Already speeding to a considerable degree, courtesy of Alby, they spend all their money on drinks at the bar whilst molesting acquaintances for a few blows on their joints. By the time the next band appears on stage they are completely ruined. Their eyes glaze and their speech becomes impossible to follow, unless you happen to be in a similar state in which case it is eminently sensible.

The whole procedure will leave them penniless, but then what is money for if not to enjoy yourself and they really don't care anyway because whatever state they find themselves in the following morning, they will carry on living and they will have had a good time.

Fran considers abusing the band that is now playing on the grounds that she isn't in it but decides not to and follows Julie to the bar instead. The bar only sells cans of lager, apart from tea which is kept boiling in a giant pot on an old cooker, incongruous in a way in the middle of the gig but at least it is something to buy which isn't illegal.

The person I've spilled my drink over is a vicious monster who shouts at me, she looks like she may well do me violence and I get ready to plead with her to stop. I'd retreat but all of a sudden I'm jammed tight with people and I can't get away. My apologies get mixed up and lost in the general noise, I'm feeling like a complete fool, why did I have to go and spill my drink and anyway why is she making such a big thing out of it? Or is it me who's making a big thing out of it? I know that everyone is looking at me and laughing to themselves, who's that hopeless incompetent throwing drink around the place, no wonder he's on his own, I mean, who'd be seen with anyone who looks like that?

"I'm sick, it's not my fault," I say in what is meant to be a placatory tone though I have to shout which ruins the effect. She still looks annoyed and gives off brutal vibrations. I seem to imagine some people lying dead around her so I offer her some speed free of charge to demonstrate what a nice person I am.

She doesn't know what speed is but she looks less annoyed so I explain that it's a drug and she asks me what it does and I try to explain but don't make a very good job of it. I take another look at my reflection and groan inside. It's hard to explain things like what things feel like to anyone else, I say to her, I was reading a book about it just the other day. This is true, I was reading a book about it.

"Spinoza?" she asks.

I look blank.

"Or Kierkegaard?"

I wonder if she is making fun of me. But she doesn't seem to be and she starts talking about the difficulty of transferring subjective impressions and such to others.

It's nice having someone to talk to now that Fran and Julie have deserted me and Jock is nowhere to be seen.

She sure knows a lot about philosophy.

June is faintly puzzled by the demeanour of the person who has spilled his drink over her. He apologises at extreme length and looks like he's in fear of his life.

He offers her some drugs for no apparent reason. She does not accept them because she does not know anything about drugs but she doesn't mind talking to him because she is lonely and he is not actually offensive in spite of the strange colour of his skin and the way he keeps glancing over his shoulder.

They get into a philosophical conversation which, while not actually inspired, is more interesting than the band that is now playing.

She talks to him for a while and then the conversation dries up and the person drifts away and June is left on her own again. For some reason she is not enjoying it, which surprises her because most of the time she is grateful for solitude.

Wu is no longer concerned about his defeat and smiles at himself for being even momentarily upset by Cheng's resounding victory. Calm after meditating, he sits in front of a blank sheet of paper with paints and brushes laid out neatly round his knees. When he feels at one with the materials he will paint a picture.

At the gig I wander away from the woman I have been talking to. She turned out to be a nice person and displayed no violence whatsoever after I apologised and what's more she knew everything there is to know about the world's philosophers. I would have liked to talk to her more but I figured that pretty soon she would get bored and I hate to talk to someone who's bored with my conversation.

In fact I get embarrassed by the thought that she might already be finding me tedious so I drift away to nowhere in particular with the vague intention of getting a cigarette off someone. I could always buy some of course, but that would mean admitting that I've failed to give up.

The band that is playing is not too interesting and I look for Fran and Julie. I see them quite close by, well it's hard not to be close by in this place, but I know by their appearance that they are beyond the communicating stage and besides they are busy kissing and I don't want to interrupt. Ferg is nowhere to be seen, I expect he found somewhere better to go, and I realise that I'm standing on my own in the middle of the hall again. It's too small a place to be wandering round like this, you keep bumping into the same people and someone's bound to get annoyed as I trample over them for the fourth time.

The music comes to an end and people start to drift away. June sees the person she was talking to shuffle past. There's a first time for everything, she thinks, and asks him home. He looks confused.

Cheng parties all night with his friends and supporters, triumphant to the point of ecstacy over his massive defeat of Wu. He is not concerned that his practising at home was in contravention of the spirit of their competition, in fact he is planning to buy more modules of different games and practise on them as well. He laughs at the thought of poor old Wu, meditating alone in his miserable little room surrounded by nothing.

Cheng and his friends celebrate in a nightclub in Soho before moving back to his flat with large amounts of alcohol, where they carry on their festivities all night long.

The person I spilled my drink over asks me home. This is such a bizarre occurrence that it nearly banishes all thought of my constant danger from my mind.

She is a nice person, but I quickly calculate what harm I can come to if I go home with her. I might get some disease. More particularly I might get AIDS, my immune system is probably not too good in the first place so I won't stand a chance.

But on the other hand I do like this girl and if I go to her flat I will be safe for a time from the killer who is after me.

I agree to go. I consider asking her if there is any chance she has AIDS. I decide against it and ask her name instead. She tells me she is called June but she doesn't ask me mine.

Outside she hails a taxi which is miraculously coming into view at this very moment, my heart sinks at the expense but she apparently senses this and says she will pay. She lives in Chelsea so I guess she can afford it.

The wife of the manager of Big Value is thinking while her husband sleeps.

She is not sorry that they will not be able to afford a Pinelog Chalet Pool because she was never very keen on the idea in the first place. She does not like to say so to her husband but she likes their back garden the way it is and does not want it occupied by a large wooden construction and anyway what good is an eighteen-foot pool to them, it's hardly room enough to swim more than a few strokes and she'd rather just go to the swimming baths. But her husband has planned to buy the deluxe model with a bar extension and then invite all his business friends over for parties. This will impress them, he thinks, swimming and saunas and cocktails, this man knows how to live.

The idea makes his wife cringe, for her opinion of his business friends is fairly low. She can imagine them all drinking too much and throwing up in the pool and quite possibly falling in and drowning.

She hates to see her husband so miserable, but no Pinelog Chalet Pool in the garden is no bad news.

I am not commonly asked home by strangers. We get to her flat in Chelsea and it is quite a wonderful place, full of philosophy books and plants. I look around casually for a mirror but I can't see one.

"There's a mirror in the bathroom," says June. I wonder if she's being sarcastic.

June makes some tea which is thoughtful of her but I drink it too quickly because I can't think of anything to say and I burn my tongue, which reminds me of an accident I had only the other day while cooking baked beans and soya burgers.

There's only one clean fork in the kitchen, all the rest of the cutlery is swilling around in the sink covered by brown evil-smelling water, so I'm using it alternately to shuffle the burgers round and stir the beans.

I put the fork in my mouth to see how the beans are getting on but I've forgotten that since removing the fork from the beans I've been poking round the frying pan at the soya burgers. When the metal touches my mouth it goes sizzle and my lips erupt with the heat, an unpleasant burning flesh smell drifts round the kitchen and I jump up and down and howl with pain.

Doctors advise running a burn under cold water for a long period of time but it's difficult to do when it's inside your mouth and after twisting around under the tap for a while I feel like I'm drowning. I look miserably at the damage in a mirror. The inside of my mouth is brown with burnt fork marks.

This has all taken quite a long time and the soya burgers catch fire but I don't want to eat them any more anyway.

This person June is a little strange, she seems to want to talk but it's all about esoteric subjects and nothing to do with what kind of music she likes and where she comes from or easy things like that.

Eventually we go to bed.

Wu wakes early and looks at the painting he
did the previous evening. He is pleased with it because it means
something to him. He wonders if he should carry on with the games
in the arcade in view of the bitterness they now cause. He used to be
friends with Cheng and now they never speak a civil word, and though
most of the antipathy comes from Cheng, Wu has to admit that he too
feels some unpleasantness.

Later today he has to go and see his teacher. He will advise him.

I worry about the divers on the seabed.

Professor Wing listens to a serious programme on the radio as he
dresses in his workman's clothes and eats as large a breakfast as he can
manage in preparation for a hard day's shovelling. Then he loads his
maps and equipment into the van and sets off for Brixton. His tent is
there as he left it, with the semicircle of orange lights warning traffic
not to drive into it and red and white bollards standing round in an

official sort of manner. Professor Wing wasn't really sure what to do with the bollards. Perhaps there is some special way of arranging them he doesn't know about? But he supposes that no one would know if he did it wrong. They stand round the tent in the pattern of Stonehenge. If an inspector happens along he can always say that they were vandalised by a local mystic cult.

Someone has drawn graffitti on the tent. It says "Janie 4 Mike". The professor winces at the use of "4" for "for" but he is pleased at the authenticity it lends to his site.

After the warning from John Primrose I know it's all true and the Milk Marketing Board is really going to rub me out, I've probably only got a few hours left, are those footsteps outside the door? They're going to kill me.

I can't imagine the world without me. It's all that newspaper reporter's fault. Why don't they kill him instead? Bastards.

A woman trained by the Brazilian secret police? My skin crawls up and down and my head tries to hide in my shoulders like a cartoon character hit on the head by a heavy weight. I try to eat something to calm my nerves but all I have in the house is a lettuce.

I hate lettuce. Every time I take some leaves off to wash them I'm terrified I'm going to find something disgusting inside like a dead wasp or a slug or maybe a severed finger or even just a fingernail. And after the trauma of washing it lettuce seems to be more or less impossible to dry, holding grimly on to water like a gigantic vegetable sponge no matter how much you shake and throw it about the kitchen, letting it out only after it squelches onto your plate. What's more it tastes of absolutely nothing and flops around in your mouth so you have to fight to get it down.

I only buy them because I think the greenstuff that they contain must be good for me and if any manufacturer is manufacturing greenstuff pills then I will certainly buy them in preference.

The day after the war in the arcade the Chinese man wants to go for a drive but Cheng does not turn up for work. Annoyed, the Chinese man phones him up to see what's wrong but Cheng does not answer. So he lets the phone ring and eventually someone does answer it, it is some stranger with a tired voice. The voice tells him to go to hell and does he know what time it is?

The Chinese man puts down the phone and thinks that if he was still working at heroin quality control in the Golden Triangle he'd have Cheng shot.

He calls up his acquaintance the detective and arranges an appointment.

I throw away the lettuce in disgust. It misses the bin and lands with a splash on the floor, the floor slopes, the water oozes out of the lettuce and runs down this slope gathering dirt to lie in a muddy puddle round the legs of the kitchen table. I ignore it. I don't care if the kitchen floor is dirty. My mother used to tell me you have to clean it every day to keep it nice, who could be bothered to clean the kitchen floor every day, all you do is walk on it.

Now I'm hungry but I'm not going out to get food, the only place around here is a chip shop that poisons its customers, they buy consignments of salmonella to add to their cooking fat, even if I made it there without getting a bullet between the eyes I'd be rushed to the hospital before the night was through and the hospital is no place to be when killers are after you, I've read *The Godfather* you know. I'll go hungry instead.

So I get down to some serious thinking about how to save my life. If this person knows my address I have to move immediately. I phone up an acquaintance who has a van and tell him to come over right away but the callous bastard says no he can't he's too busy and he can't make it till tomorrow morning.

"You'll be fucking sorry when I'm dead," I say. He doesn't reply.

"Where are you going?" he wants to know. I don't know, I tell him, just turn up tomorrow and we'll go there.

The manager of Big Value is arriving wearily at his store for another day's work. He used to be in early every day, even at weekends, but recently he has become disheartened by his poor results. He no longer greets the women who work behind the cash registers which is a relief to them, now they only have the security guard to worry about.

The chief security guard is in conference with the other security staff, uniformed and plain clothes.

"We'd better start catching some people," he says. "Our jobs are in danger. The manager was moaning at me yesterday." They all say yes they'll do their best to catch some shoplifters.

Fran wanders in.

She has not been to sleep because she took too much speed the night before and it kept her awake despite all the other drugs she took. So she said to Julie, who didn't sleep either, that she would go out and get them some breakfast.

She picks up a basket and examines the shelves.

I knew where I could move to because someone I knew had just moved out of her squat on a council estate. I spent the rest of the evening packing my stuff and listening to DBC. DBC stands for Dread Broadcasting Corporation and is a pirate reggae station.

An' DBC keep you rockin' an' ting.

They got reggae and African music and some old rhythm and blues and it is generally a wonderful station, as well as playing music they advertise gigs and events and where to buy the latest style in hats, this being Big Apple in Acre Lane, crammed to the roof with fashionable headware. Sometimes they go off the air altogether, this is one of the risks of being a pirate.

It doesn't take long to pack my belongings because I have pathetically little apart from my vast horde of comics which I store with loving care in cardboard boxes I have been saving for just such an emergency. Well I wasn't actually expecting to be on someone's hit list but a sudden move is always possible with the amount of people that don't like me, someone is always taking a dislike to me for some spurious reason or other, when I feel bad I think I'm the world's most unpopular person. When I feel good I don't mind so much that I am. The only reason that anyone speaks to me at all is that I bring them amphetamines.

I tell the hamster that we have to move but reassure him that I'll make sure his house is carried with special care and he'll hardly notice a thing. I promise to buy him some Malteesers to make up for the inconvenience.

When DBC comes to an end around one in the morning I switch over and listen to some news and I hear that it's not the seabed at all that the divers are staging their sit-in on, it's an oil rig. I'm relieved for their sake, though I wouldn't fancy hanging round unnecessarily on an oil rig either, these thing collapse and sink at the slightest excuse.

Professor Wing is digging away. Every so often he seeks reassurance from the maps which are concealed in the pockets of his stolen donkey jacket. Although he is fairly sure that he is digging in the right place he has no idea how far down the crown is buried because none of the documents mentioned the depth, not even the important one inside the *Beano* annual.

His colleague at work was immensely grateful for the *Beano* annual. Now he has only one left to collect for a complete set.

The professor becomes aware that there is somebody standing close by and immediately worries in case it is a council inspector. He tries to make his digging look more professional and mentally polishes up his explanation as to why he is there on his own. Government cutbacks, he's going to say to anyone who asks, we're only allowed one man per hole these days.

But when he looks up he finds it's not a council inspector, it's a black woman of about forty. He assumes that a forty-year-old black woman is not going to be a council roadworks inspector, not in Britain she isn't.

She gives him a cheery greeting and tells him that he should be careful if he comes across anything unusual while he is digging. "I think there's a valuable old crown buried round here somewhere," she says, "a relic from the time of Ethelred the Unready."

This person arrived the next morning as arranged and I immediately moaned at him because he was ten minutes late.

"Well what difference does it make?"

I just give him a filthy look and get down to the business of loading up my stuff.

"I'll carry my comics and you carry everything else," I tell him. This is not unreasonable as my comic collection is considerably larger than all the rest of my possessions put together.

After a while of straining up and down stairs we've got all my clothes and records and various other things packed but there are still a lot of comics left. Reluctantly I let him help with these in the interests of speed but I keep a close watch on him to make sure he doesn't pocket any.

Almost immediately he picks up a box without due care and attention.

"Don't bump them," I shout.

"For fuck's sake, it's only a box of comics."

"Well it might only be a box of comics to you you fucking moron but they're worth a lot to me and just make sure you're careful with them."

We carry on, both annoyed.

I'm in constant fear that the next corner I turn I'm going to walk into the killer and that will be the end of me, and this fear aggravates my annoyance at the utter lack of care being shown by this meathead who's helping me move.

My guts start to hurt.

I get down to the van and my helper is putting something in his pocket.

"I saw that you bastard," I scream. "You've stolen a comic. Put it back or I'll kill you." I look menacing.

He looks bemused but he's not fooling me. I lunge at him and grapple his hand out of his pocket.

There isn't any comic there. He must have sneaked it back.

Professor Wing is appalled. He doesn't know what to say. How does this woman know about the crown? Who is she to just come along and casually announce that she thinks there might be something valuable in the area?

"Crown?" he mumbles. "Crown?"

"Yes," she replies. "An old crown lost at the time of Ethelred the Unready, though to tell you the truth I don't know when Ethelred the Unready lived. I wonder why he was called the Unready?"

Professor Wing knows but he is not going to give himself away by telling. It seems that this woman takes him for a genuine road digger so things may still go to plan. The crown was old and valuable even in Ethelred's day, and no one is going to stop Professor Wing discovering it if he has any say in the matter.

"How do you know about this crown?" His voice sounds weak. "A local Brixton legend?"

"No, I read about it in the public library. It didn't actually say where it was but I'm psychic and I do a bit of divination, I'm pretty sure it's round here somewhere."

Professor Wing is momentarily impressed by this startling new evidence for the validity of paranormal phenomena but he gets over it quickly.

"Well, I must get back to digging," he says to her, feigning boredom. "There's only me here, it's the cuts you know."

"Sure," she says. "I'll just hang around and try to pin-point the exact location."

The professor is miserable but keeps on digging.

Fran does not realise that she is not functioning at maximum efficiency. Drugs are still rampaging around her body. Normally her complete confidence that she will not be caught serves to protect her but today she is being followed by a store detective who is determined to catch somebody as a safeguard against losing her job.

Fran would usually sense the presence of a store detective but her senses aren't working too well, she can't even make up her mind about what to steal. Eventually she makes her selection and wanders towards one of the checkout points. She is going to pay for a small tin of beans. Inside her clothes she bulges with stolen goods.

The detective follows her.

She pays for the beans and steps outside. She feels a hand on her shoulder and it is a store detective asking her to step back inside.

Oh fuck, thinks Fran.

The Chinese man has contacted the detective and put the matter in his hands. He knows that the detective will find Alby Starvation easily enough. He wonders what has happened to Cheng, but when he leaves his house and walks through Soho he learns of Cheng's victory over Wu the previous night. Everyone is talking about it. People are saying they never saw poor old Wu or his supporters so downcast.

So the Chinese man guesses that Cheng is probably still sleeping due to excessive celebrating, and though for the life of him he cannot see that it is all that much to celebrate about he does know how important it is to Cheng. And as a happy Cheng is an efficient Cheng, he does not mind too much.

I accuse this cretin of deliberately dropping a box of comics and we almost come to blows. It seems to me he's deliberately trying to damage them, he gets within ten feet of the *Silver Surfer* I attack him.

Finally we get everything in the van, I sit protectively over the comics. He slams the door and starts the engine.

"Don't go too fast," I tell him. I direct him to the new residence of the girl whose ex-squat I intend to hide in. When we get there he wants to wait outside but I don't trust him not to drive away and I make him follow me inside.

I beg the key off the girl. She was intending to give it to another friend who needs a place to stay but after I rant for a while about all the people who are trying to kill me she gives in and gives it to me. Anyway, I say, if you don't I'll just go and jemmy the door open.

When we get to the new place we start to unload and start to argue. He wants some more money for petrol, mean bastard I think, and give him the coins in my pocket, we argue some more about transporting the comics and everything into the new flat, the neighbours look out their windows, Jesus not more squatters they think, why doesn't the council board up that place and give us some peace?

The van driver says he never wants to see me again. Well that's fine with me, I tell him, and scan the front seat for anything he may have hidden. He goes away. I lock the door and go to buy some sweets for Happy.

But just as the store detective is on the point of hauling Fran back inside the shop there is a mad commotion behind them and two figures burst out of the shop door, struggling and kicking. One of the figures is wearing a blue uniform with white trimmings while the other is dressed in a grey suit. They plunge through a pile of discarded cardboard boxes into a mountain of wire baskets which topples in several directions to crash onto the open vegetable stalls which line the pavement in front of Big Value. Carrots and onions and potatoes fall in an avalanche and roll under the feet of the quickly gathering crowd of spectators.

The security guard is having a hard time in the fight. The cashier women come running out to root for his opponent.

The store detective lets go of Fran and advances hesitantly to help the guard. Not unreasonably she is wary of being kicked by a stray foot. Fran takes the opportunity to slip away, still carrying the stolen goods. As she walks off she hears a voice emerging from the struggle.

"Let me go, I'm an executive with the Milk Marketing Board!"

Once in my new flat I stopped all contact with newspapers and television and radio and most people I knew.

I go to ground and worry.

I consider applying for police protection or exposing the Milk Marketing Board to the BBC but decide against both on the grounds that no one would believe me. But I know I can't hide forever, in fact I probably can't hide for very long at all.

I decide on a policy of militant defence and pick up my copy of *The Godfather* to look for some tips. There doesn't seem time to recruit a large family however, so I decide that I will get myself a weapon. This will cost a lot of money and my only asset is my comic collection. The only way I can defend myself is by selling my comics.

I wonder if anyone ever suffered as much.

Wu arrives at his teacher's flat which is as barely furnished as his own. His teacher already knows all about last night's happenings and, as he can see in Wu's face, that he wants advice so he gives him his opinion.

"Carry on with the games," he says. "How is your painting coming on?"

They drink tea for a while, and discuss painting.

I'm going back to Brixton the next day after sleeping with June. She told me I am the most ragged person she has ever met and gave me a pair of army trousers she doesn't want any more. She still seems to quite like me.

Although I'm feeling better that somebody likes me I'm feeling worse because tomorrow I have to see this Pamela Patterson person, a person with comics to sell who I know in reality is a killer who is going to eradicate me as the final solution to the poor sales figures.

So I have to think of some plan to save myself. I wish I had a gun but I don't and even if I do manage to somehow escape from her then there is still this Chinese man in hot pursuit. A few minutes thinking about these matters brings on an attack of extreme insecurity and I have trouble crossing the road. Some people can cope with all of life's dangers no trouble at all but they certainly got me beat. I hang around town for a while not knowing what to do, whether to go home or maybe just get on an aeroplane and fly to Morocco. But I don't have any money and anyway I'm scared of aeroplanes, besides they would only follow me, sadistic bastards.

I start to worry in case anyone is making off with my comics through a hole in the ceiling and this hurries me home. My hamster is a loyal friend but he's just too small to protect the flat from burglars.

Fran and Julie are eating breakfast in a desultory manner, now that they have food they don't seem to be hungry. This happens frequently and they are both becoming rather thin; if there were more calories in drugs it might help.

Fran recounts her close escape to Julie. "A near thing," she says. "That detective that grabbed me was probably trained to restrain shoplifters by force, if that fight hadn't broken out she'd have had me in a headlock till the police arrived."

"Does that mean we can't get food from Big Value any more?"

Fran isn't sure, she might be recognised and followed by the detective if she goes back. This annoys her no end as she has never had any trouble before in any shop during many years of liberating goods, and Big Value is the most convenient place for her to go. Still, there are plenty of shops in Brixton.

"We're Backing Brixton," they say as part of their advertising campaign, well that's fine with Fran so long as she doesn't actually have to spend any money in them.

Back at the store the man in the grey suit has been restrained and bundled into the small security room at the rear. The man in the grey suit is Withers, second in command of the Milk Marketing Board's dirty tricks department. He is protesting his innocence and saying he did not mean to walk out of the store with a tin of strawberries in his hand but this will not do him any good, We Always Prosecute say the signs around the walls and they mean it, don't try telling us you did it by accident we get your kind in here every day.

Withers didn't mean to do it. He is suffering from attacks of absent-mindedness brought on by nerves and pressure of work stemming directly from the poor sales figures up and down the country.

Almost nobody drinks milk any more.

The woman has wandered off round the corner and Professor Wing is digging away furiously. He does not know what to do. He cannot try to discourage her in any manner for fear of giving himself away. The only thing to do is to find the crown quickly before she complicates matters any further.

How could she possibly divine its presence? After all his work and study, she just comes along and guesses where it is? She doesn't even know when Ethelred the Unready lived for Christ's sake, what right has she got to barge into the situation like this? Damnation, he thinks, and keeps on digging. He comes to some earth like concrete and manhandles his drill into position. He hates to use the drill because it vibrates through his hands and body and feels always like it's on the verge of going out of control.

He switches it on and plunges it into the earth. There is a crunching noise and a few shards of some red material fly past his face followed immediately by a jet of water. Jesus, thinks the professor, I've burst a water pipe.

The water gurgles out and over his stolen council issue shoes.

When I first moved into my new squat I spent a lot of time sitting being miserable.

Listening to my reggae records helps a bit but not a lot when I'm walking round looking at the plastered-up holes in the ceiling through which at any moment a large gang of criminals is going to burst waving knives and razors prior to attacking and robbing me and leaving me holding my head together in a pool of blood on the kitchen floor, if I had any money I'd move somewhere, anywhere, and get the entire house covered in a steel casing with just one door which would open only to my fingerprints and voice pattern so I could feel safe from the world. However, this place would probably lead to severe attacks of claustrophobia and perhaps the only solution is to move to a desert island somewhere and eke out an existence among the palm trees. But I have read that often people get killed sitting under palm trees when coconuts fall on their heads. This is the sort of thing they don't tell you in these theology books about the ordered creation of the universe as death by falling coconut is difficult to square with a universe creator of high intelligence.

I want to get advice from somebody. I'd like to see my friend Stacey but he is seriously ill in a hospital after contracting tetanus from a dirty vitamin C tablet, he comes in and out of a coma and rants about the dangers of health food shops.

And even if by some miracle the burglars don't get me then the hitperson will, I worry myself into a frenzy, my only comfort is talking to the hamster and he can't think of a solution either. It's around this time that I got to hear about this Chinese man who's been looking for me.

The Chinese man is sitting around in his office doing big business over the telephone, he's got a line to Burma and a line to New York, he's arranging a big heroin deal which will net a fantastic amount of money for him, also for a few others.

This money will unfortunately not get him the woman of his dreams and he still seems no nearer to marrying into the English aristocracy, his ultimate ambition. Then perhaps he could be an earl or a lord or something, his knowledge of the English aristocracy is lacking in detail, in fact the only ones he ever sees are the drunken wretches at his nightclub. Still, they can't all be like that, for one thing it would be too dangerous when shooting grouse. Or should that be grice? Whatever the plural is, can you be drunk when you shoot them?

It is hard for normal people to know things like that.

I get home after sleeping with June. Tomorrow I'm meeting with Pamela Patterson. I haven't managed to get hold of a gun, I haven't even found out where you get one, in America you just walk into the local post office or iron-mongers and buy one over the counter. An M16? Certainly, sir, will I wrap it or do you want to use it now?

I put on a tape I've made from reggae on the radio.

The girls them a watch me,

They jus' a watch me.

Arrogant bastard, I think, but it is a good record. I dance distractedly around the house searching for inspiration. I have to meet this woman in a pub at lunchtime, well at least she can't shoot me on the spot, there again I can hardly club her to death on the premises either. My only advantage is that she doesn't know that I know who she really is.

I'm not thinking about where I'm dancing and I take a wrong turn out of the bedroom and smash my skin into a chair, what the fuck is that chair doing there, no one sits in the hall do they?

Mashing up your shin on a surprise chair is agonisingly painful and I sit down to moan.

The manager of Big Value is delighted to be face to face with one of the shoplifters who have been pillaging his store.

"You bastard," he screams at Withers. "You've been robbing us blind and now you're going to pay." He hits him in the mouth. "What did you do with the gas fire you took?"

Withers looks shocked and bemused. The manager hits him again.

"How many tins of strawberries have you taken?"

Withers tries to protest that he's never stolen anything from this or any other store but the security guards are massed in a circle around him and they look menacing.

"We want a full confession out of you before we call the police," the manager tells him. "And you're not getting out of here till we get it." He slaps him for the third time. "How did you get rid of the goods?"

After the non-breakfast Julie leaves the house to go to her women's self-defence class. She is still not too steady on her feet after the night before but she thinks she will be fine by the time she gets there, well she had better be because her teacher does not like anyone just going through the motions.

The class is held in the gigantic basement of a squat nearby. The building used to be an army careers office and the giant basement was earmarked as a nuclear shelter but the office was closed in a regional reshuffle of army careers offices, the building was too old and lacked sufficient window space for displaying model tanks and soldiers and signs saying come in and see us.

Everyone else is there by the time Julie arrives and she joins in as the class warms up. As soon as she does her first stretching exercise she feels like she's going to throw up, as far as she can remember this has never happened in class before.

In the hospital Stacey is really ill. He should be in the intensive therapy unit but it is full up so he is lying on a bed in what used to be the stationery store because it is quite close by. He has contracted tetanus and also a mystery illness, the doctors are not sure what it is. He contracted tetanus from this dirty vitamin C tablet because it had been stored next to some organically grown carrots in a health food shop and the organically grown carrots had spewed dirt over most of the shelf.

Now he drifts in and out of his coma and rambles into space. He is completely incoherent.

I make it out of hiding across the road to the park one Saturday because there is a festival being held there, it is organised by CND and I feel I should support it on principle besides I wanted to see the bands and I suppose that in amongst all these thousands of people I'll be safe enough.

So I wander over and the park is absolutely full of millions of young people all not minding too much that the weather is threatening to wash us away and taking advantage of the occasion to show off their new hair colours to everyone including the police with binoculars high above on the surrounding rooftops.

The festival is fun with foodstalls and badges and kiddie entertainments and old clothes and books and small political parties and everything would seem not too bad were it not for the fact that all those young people make me feel old, I'm sure some of them are laughing quietly as I go by.

I keep my head rotating as if constantly looking for someone so no one can focus on my wrinkles and when the DJ plays old records from my childhood I pretend convincingly to myself that I've never heard them before, in fact I deliberately look puzzled as each record comes on so people will see I don't know what it is.

Professor Wing reacts quickly to the calamity and wraps his jacket round the pipe to halt the flow while he rushes off to his van to hunt for some more permanent means of repair. There is a box marked emergency supplies in the back of the van but all it contains is bandages. There doesn't seem to be anything suitable for mending burst water pipes. He doesn't really know what you do use for mending burst water pipes.

In desperation he grabs the bandages and hurries back, water is already seeping through the jacket and trickling over onto the earth, at least the hole is covered by the workman's tent so no one can see what has happened, not for a while anyway, not till the street floods.

He has to put his hands underwater to reach the bottom of the pipe and it is freezing cold. He wraps all of the bandages round as tight as he can and it seems to stop the flow. He supposes that if he had some tar or something that he could coat the bandages with it might effect a reasonable repair, but he does not have any tar and he sees no prospect of getting any, as far as he knows tar is not a commodity you can buy in the shops.

Extremely disturbed by the accident, an unlooked for occurrence which has emphasised how unused to and unprepared for this manner of work he is, worried about the black woman who threatens to ruin his exclusive discovery, he gets back to digging. At least the water has softened the earth.

The black woman is called Muriel.

She is reading a book about historical treasures in Britain that she has borrowed from the library and when she comes to this reference about a crown she has an extraordinarily strong feeling that it is somewhere nearby. All the book says is that this fantastically old and valuable crown was lost around the time of King Ethelred the Unready somewhere in the south of England. No more information is provided but it is enough for Muriel. She is psychic and frequently has odd notions which prove to be well-founded.

So she puts on her coat and walks out on the street to follow her senses. When she arrives at what seems to be the source of the signal she finds a workman in close proximity. He gives off pretty strange signals himself but she does not think too much about it at the time. She exchanges a few words with him before trying to pinpoint the crown's exact location. She doesn't know what she will do if it turns out to be buried under a block of flats.

Oh shit, it's almost tomorrow and that could well be the last day of my life, in fact it's looking increasingly likely, I mean what chance have I got against this killer, absolutely none I would think. I haven't told the hamster about meeting this so-called Pamela Patterson because I don't want to worry him too much but I have made provisions for someone to look after him if anything happens to me, an old girlfriend I'm still friends with, well at least she doesn't actively dislike me, just give him lots of food including plenty of chocolate and he'll be fine, I tell her, I know it will be all right because she has much experience of hamstercare.

I pace the rooms endlessly and I don't get any sleep and somehow I can't quite figure out how any of this happened, I mean is it normal for people to be after you with guns and things? No I don't think so, well it never seems to happen to anyone else I know. I stare wild-eyed at my comics and think how they might suffer without anyone to look after them. Who will dust them and shuffle them round with loving care? Who will buy the latest numbers? What will happen to my complete *Thor*?

Then I feel annoyed at them for being so difficult to sell. How can you sell something as awkward as a comic collection, it would have been all right if that person with the van who moved my stuff had been a reasonable human being then he could have helped me again but really he was a complete moron and if I never see him again then that will be just fine.

There's not that many reasonable human beings about, you know.

By force of will Julie manages not to be sick. She stretches for a while on her own before lining up with the rest of the class in front of the teacher to follow her movements and instructions.

When someone does a move badly the instructor bawls at her. The class's instructor is a woman from Hong Kong. She arrived in Britain only a year ago on the run from the authorities in Burma after the warlord for whom she was a bodyguard was gunned down by the army in an operation against heroin production and trafficking. Now she teaches kung fu to women in south London.

Withers, the second in command of the Milk Marketing Board's dirty tricks department, is still being questioned by the manager of Big Value.

"You bastard," snarls Withers as the manager hits him again, "I'll get you for this, when my department gets to work on you you'll be lucky to escape with your life."

But the manager does not listen because all he can think of is the Pinelog Chalet Pool he is not going to get for his back garden and the executive parties he will not be able to hold and the fact that he cannot get promoted out of this hole because the majority of his stock disappears into space.

The security guards take their jackets off.

"We've got all day, sunshine," they say. "Now, are you going to sign this confession or do we have to persuade you some more?"

The detective hired by the Chinese man to find the sulphate dealer in Brixton completes his task in no time at all. He phones up the Chinese man and tells him Alby's new address, thank you says the Chinese man and writes out a cheque to pay him with. He wonders what time will be best for getting in touch. Business commitments keep him busy for the rest of the day, there always seem to be more drugs coming into the country or more people to bribe or the occasional job of frightening to be done, it is no bed of roses being a big-time criminal in a strange country, sometimes he thinks were it not for the incentives he gets from the government as a small business he would give up altogether and take up language teaching full time.

Well, in between then and now I didn't do much but hide and things. I give up public life altogether.

WHERE IS THE MILK CAMPAIGNER? asks a newspaper, but I stay underground apart from collecting and delivering the odd gram of sulphate and I only do that to keep my friends.

It distresses me staying hidden because I have several big comic deals in the air. At the last comic fair I organised several transactions through a dealer I know. He was going to introduce me to another collector who is eager to swap me some old *Iron Man*s for some rare *Spiderman* duplicates I have tucked away. Oh well.

But I know all the time that matters will come to a head. I hope I don't get sick because my doctor is bound to be in on the plot, one visit to him and he'll be hot on the phone to the Milk Marketing Board, here he is, come and get him but take care not to harm the *Silver Surfer*, he promised them to me.

I hate my doctor.

Muriel walks back to the roadworks. She is going to tell the workman the good news that, as far as she can tell, the crown is located directly beneath his site. She hopes that he will be pleased to hear this and will go easy on the power drilling for fear of breaking the relic in half, but she is not confident about this as when she mentioned it to him before he did not seem very interested. She supposes that he is having to work very hard because of the cuts in public services, it's not often you see a lone worker digging up the road.

"Hello," she shouts into the orange and white striped tent. A worried looking face appears. Muriel tells him that she thinks the crown is directly below. But he does not react, just grunts and disappears.

Muriel senses that all is not what it seems.

Cheng wakes eventually with a massive hangover. His vision is so bad that he is not sure at first if his eyes are open. He feels terrible and wonders whose is this other body lying in the hall beside him. It grunts and shivers as he stumbles to his feet. Satisfied that it is not a corpse Cheng shuffles onward, ignoring the body along with all other remnants of last night's party.

There is another stranger in his kitchen but Cheng feels too ill to object, the light shining through the window pierces his eyes painfully, yes, they definitely are open, he thinks.

He wonders what to do. But the wondering hurts too much so he sits down next to the stranger on the kitchen chair. An ashtray full way beyond overflowing looms up into his face in a nauseating fashion so he knocks it off the table onto the floor. He sits and waits for the hangover to pass.

During this time I was hiding in the house I listen to the radio in between reggae records and consequently amass a vast store of general knowledge, for instance, talking bus stops to help the blind, a fine idea it seems to me, the oil rig sit-in continues, my sympathies are firmly with the workers and it will not surprise me if the oil company torpedoes the rig, a vicious wild animal is stalking Dartmoor savaging sheep and lambs and pigs and anything else unfortunate enough to cross its path at mealtimes, a regiment of marines are out looking for it with orders to shoot to kill which will push up the mortality rate for moors walkers but that doesn't worry me so long as they kill it before it changes its hunting ground to Brixton, I've got enough problems without a mad beast eating me for breakfast.

More of my hair falls out and I age about a year every day.

On one of my rare trips out of the house I'm down at Fran and Julie's and I'm moaning in an entirely reasonable manner about my troubles when Fran tells me I complain too much.

I'm incredulous. "What, me?"

"Yes," she says. "You're always whining and looking miserable, why not look on the bright side for a change and try bringing a little happiness into the world?"

I consider what she says and find that I can't really deny it. I am always miserable.

So I resolve to change. From now on it's no more complaints from Alby.

There's a hired killer out to shoot me! There's a Chinese gangster after me! I'm getting old and I'm always ill! It's great! It's fun time down here in sweltering sun-drenched Brixton, no more complaints from me!

I go away resolving determinedly to be more cheerful.

Stacey wakes up and moans.

"Muriel," he says.

Muriel is the name of a nurse who is nice to him when she has the time, which is not too often. He lapses back into his coma, lying quietly in his bed in what used to be the stationery store.

Julie feels better after the class, blood begins to circulate which gives her an appetite and sends her home for a second try at breakfast.

"Hello Fran, you wanna eat anything?"

They make a meal and after they've eaten it they discuss what they're going to do tonight and how they're going to do it.

"Do we have any sulphate left?"

"No."

"Any grass?"

"No."

"Anything?"

"No."

"Any money? No. Do you think we could trade any of this food you stole for some drugs?"

They consider it. Where can you trade stolen food for drugs? They're not sure, but it seems like a good idea. After all, you can't go to a club or a party clutching a loaf of bread.

Sometimes I programme my drum machine and play along guitar to it. I wanna play in a band but every time I play with some other people they turn out to be utter morons without talent or intelligence, out of jealousy or stupidity they spoil the good things I come up with. Bastards. It would not be so bad if they were reasonable human beings but they never are, in my experience musicians are the scum of the earth, all ego and nothing else, if I had enough money I'd hire a studio and do the entire record myself and it would turn out pretty damn good, I can tell you.

Professor Wing is having difficulties. Water keeps seeping out of the pipe and nothing he can do will stop it. He is scared to use the drill any more in case he gets electrocuted, in fact with so much water running around and electric cables no doubt somewhere in the near vicinity, electrocution seems like a real possibility, drill or no drill. But he is determined not to give up because he is convinced that if he does, then the woman will reappear seconds after his departure and will probably find the crown just inches away from where he left off.

He still can't believe his misfortune. How could this woman possibly have just happened along today?

The reason she happened along today is that the crown is magic and gives off signals, which are amplified by the professor's strong feelings on the subject.

I'm sitting looking out of the window on my last night on earth.

It's an awful place but where else is there to go? Outside my window the weather is miserable and it makes the drab scenery worse. Out in the darkness I imagine a mystery killer beast prowling around eating things, bored with life on Dartmoor it has prowled its way down to Brixton to terrorise the council estates. I worry in case I dropped a glove or something out on the street and it finds it and decides my scent is particularly appetising and is at this moment tracking me down prior to eating me.

Where is Dartmoor? Is it far from Brixton? I worry in case the marines follow it down and kill me by mistake with a stray bullet through the window. I sometimes worry about a stray bullet coming through the window, I expect lots of people do.

Tomorrow I'm going to hand my head on a plate to a fiend in human shape, namely Pamela Patterson, the bogus comic seller who is in reality a hitperson trained in Brazil and capable of tearing me apart with her bare hands.

I wander gloomily into the bedroom and consider making a last-minute bolt for freedom. But I'd have to leave my comics to the mercy of every thieving vulture in London and I can't bear the thought of that and anyway my enemies would only track me down. The Milk Marketing Board is having the stations watched, I expect, he's on the 9.23 to Manchester, send out the squad to dynamite the track.

What will happen if I manage to defeat Pamela Patterson? Will they leave me alone now that I've been out of the headlines for a while?

Well they might, but wild optimism does not course through my veins.

Withers has been beaten into signing the confession and is now languishing in a small prison cell in Brixton police station along with two other people.

"How many times you been in a cell, Jock?" asks Sanny.

Jock shakes his head. "Canny count them. How about you?"

"Me neither."

Withers tries to ignore them. He has confessed to organising a large-scale criminal organisation responsible for mass outbreaks of shoplifting at Big Value, yes it was me, he was forced to say, I was the criminal mastermind behind the gang, we stole from your shelves then fenced the stuff through London to other crooked shopkeepers, I had twenty-five people on the payroll and we've been operating for the past two years. The pressure of work at the Milk Marketing Board drove him to it.

But now he is thinking with great clarity and is planning to revenge himself on the manager of Big Value in some appalling manner which will involve ruining his career at the very least and may well stretch to physical damage. No one messes with a member of the dirty tricks department, he thinks, not if they know what's good for them.

Wu walks for a while through the streets where he lives. He arrives at the small area of grass that makes up Soho square where he sits down to watch the people around him eating lunch.

Generally the people eating lunch here are free from work for their lunchbreak and seem pretty happy about it and this small pleasure is interesting to watch. A few yards up the road is Oxford Street where anyone feeling happy would be a rare occurrence as they push and shove their way along the crowded pavements past junk-ridden shops all the while being seriously damaged by the fumes from the extraordinarily large amount of taxis that crawl along the street past windows full of sloganised T-shirts that surround the windows of large department stores struggling to get with the beat of today's modern culture.

Oxford Street, thinks Wu, is more or less the nadir of Western civilisation.

Meanwhile Cheng, being a fairly healthy sort of person, is recovering rapidly from his hangover and regaining his good spirits. He is still triumphant from last night's victory and knows that when he sees his friends they will congratulate him again.

He intends to call again at the video store to buy another game module, he will find out what is going to be the next popular one and get some practice in quick. And as soon as he can empty his flat of the remnants of last night's party he is going to practice again at Kill Another One. They will be playing that for a while yet and he relishes the thought of more victories over Wu, he hates Wu, he hates him bitterly.

Then Cheng remembers that he is meant to be working today and groans, he is already very late and his employer is highly intolerant. He tries to get ready but he is hampered by the still-sleeping bodies scattered throughout the flat, he cannot go out to work leaving strangers in his place so he wakes and ejects them.

Jesus Christ I look worse all the time, why the fuck did whoever decorated this poxy flat put mirrors all over the fucking place? Were they deliberately trying to make me feel bad?

I'm a hopeless mirror addict, I can't go past one without stopping to have a look and the outcome is always depressing. Mirrors seem to me to be malicious objects that are out to make me feel bad. I certainly don't believe they're as objective as they're made out to be.

I don't bother trying to sleep, it's better to spend the night worrying in bed, the radio is pumping out news and I'm surprised how little there seems to be. The same things are endlessly recycled and if a truckload of porridge is spilled on the A4 you can be sure you'll hear about it four times an hour for a day and a half.

The night passes with such slowness as to defy description.

At her home up in north London, Pamela Patterson goes to bed. Beside her bed there is a pile of comics which she is going to sell tomorrow to some person in Brixton. She will be sad to sell them even though they are all spare copies and they will raise her a lot of money. Real comic fans don't like letting a comic go in any circumstances.

June has mixed feelings after sleeping with the person she met at the gig.

He seemed like a reasonable sort of person and it has cured the loneliness which has temporarily affected her, but it has meant sacrificing some of her privacy which she resents. She wouldn't exactly say she's had a great time but there again she hasn't had a terrible time either. Noisier than a book and slightly less fun.

She did not find out his name and does not expect to see him again. Though he had seemed to want to meet her again June did not encourage him.

At times she got the impression that his mind was somewhere else.

Her thoughts turn to her current contract, the person in Brixton she is due to kill. Her mind dwells on it for a little while in the bath. After her bath June wanders around the flat watering all the various plants that spread out over the walls and floor to give a hanging garden effect that she finds comforting. She does not talk to them because in her experience it does not make any difference.

Cheng, still slightly bedraggled, has arrived at his employer's house to report for work. He is very late and, as expected, his employer is not at all amused, in fact he lectures Cheng for some considerable time about how if circumstances were different Cheng would at this very moment be looking for alternative employment. Still, the Chinese man is not as annoyed as he pretends to be because he knows the reason for Cheng's lateness and does not altogether disapprove because he has met Wu and didn't like him either. Wu gave him the distinct impression that he disapproved of him, and who was he, a pseudo little mystic, to disapprove of someone who used to run the heroin quality control department for a warlord in the Golden Triangle?

He tells Cheng that he has located Alby Starvation and that they will be visiting him soon, though not today because there is much else to do.

There is a magazine lying open on the desk displaying classified adverts. Cheng asks his employer if he is looking for somewhere else to live because he knows a good property dealer. His employer frowns at him and closes the magazine.

Professor Wing is defeated. Water flows freely out of the pipe and forces him back to the surface. He is at a loss, his academic training has just not equipped him to deal with such a situation. No doubt a genuine road digger could effect an immediate and permanent repair but no doubt a genuine road digger would not have burst the pipe in the first place.

What can he do now? He can't go and report it to the water authorities or they will start asking awkward questions like "What are you, a complete imposter, doing digging up the country's roads?" They will demand to know who he is, hand him over to the police, expose him to ridicule in front of the entire academic world. He can imagine the headlines in both the serious and popular press, stories mocking him for trying to keep the discovery to himself, laughing at him for his efforts at manual labour, puns about floods of knowledge.

And then there is the matter of the material borrowed from the British Library, material which could be construed, by those unsympathetic to his cause, as stolen.

Temporarily nonplussed, he stands in his tent and watches the water rise.

Well, even if I could sell my comic collection now it is too late to convert the profit into a pump action shotgun so that plan is out the window for the meantime.

Pamela Patterson.

I'm starting to freeze with terror. I wish that I could be catapulted into an alternative universe in an amazing accident.

Pamela Patterson.

Towards dawn it suddenly seems like a good idea for the night to pass slowly, but it seems to have sped up and despite all my efforts to prevent it, morning arrives.

I'm struck with a feeling of morbid horror and sympathy for anyone spending their last night in a condemned cell before being taken away in the morning to be executed, how do you manage to stay sane when you know that the next morning someone is going to come and take you and strap you into an electric chair or stand you on a gallows or up against a wall and no matter how ridiculous or unreasonable it seems and no matter how much you want the situation to just go away and leave you alone it won't and come daylight you are shivering with fear, surely there must be some way out of this, in life there is always some alternative action you can take but this time there is not and all you can do is try to melt into the wall when they come for you, your legs just give way on this last walk and you start to cry because that is all your body can do in protest at what they are going to do to it?

The manager of Big Value is writing out a report to send to head office. In the report he tells how through the diligence of himself and the security staff a large organised gang of shoplifters has been routed. The matter is now in the hands of the police, he writes, who confidently expect to clear up the rest of the gang and bring to an end a network of organised crime that stretched from Brixton to the south of France. He also writes enthusiastically that figures will now show a marked improvement, and in an outburst of happiness he phones his wife to tell her the good news.

"I might make my bonus after all," he enthuses. "And then we'll be able to afford the Chalet Pool."

His wife is appalled but hides it well. He tells her that they will go out to dinner tonight by way of celebration and she pretends to be enthusiastic about this too, although she has already begun to prepare their evening meal.

She looks forward to a life of cooking snacks for his business friends while they lounge around the pool getting drunk.

I had an unfortunate accident when I was born. The doctor dropped me on my head. Here we are, he was saying, a healthy baby boy, when I slipped through his fingers and thumped onto the floor. He was dangling me upside down at the time, a dangerous practice you would think but something that is apparently often done with babies. So my first contact with the world was a blow on the head and I still remember the incident. One moment I'm happily curled up in warm peaceful surroundings, the next I'm dive-bombing the floor.

I've always thought that it was deliberate. Even at that age people didn't like me. I would have sued for malpractice but I hadn't yet learned to speak and I suppose that now it is too late.

And while this incident might have been responsible for my gigantic intelligence, I feel that it may have had something to do with my consequent emotional problems. And what use is it being cleverer than everyone else if you're miserable all the time?

Defeated, at least for the moment, Professor Wing beats a tactical retreat, placing all his equipment as casually as he can in his van before driving off home to consider the matter. He has some idea of gathering materials and effecting a repair—he could probably get a book from the public library which would instruct him on how to do it—but in view of the fact that very soon someone is going to notice major flooding in the vicinity he is a bit wary of returning.

When he reaches home he parks the van in the garage and goes inside to pace up and down and worry. One minute the crown was more or less in his grasp, now it is seemingly unobtainable. He looks glumly at his assembly of maps, parchments, and ancient manuscripts and begins to regret not going about things in the proper manner. If he had, then he would not have been able to keep the discovery of the crown exclusively to himself, but he would not have had to flee the scene when things went wrong.

They never had this sort of trouble in the Valley of the Kings, he thinks. There they could hack and dig away to their hearts' content, secure in the knowledge that no matter what happened they wouldn't be flooded out by a thoughtlessly placed water pipe.

Muriel goes back to the tent for a third time. She intends to say goodbye to the workman, but when she gets there she notices that water is beginning to lap out from the front flap of the tent.

She shouts but gets no reply.

Worried in case there has been an accident she steps through the bollards and warning lights and opens the flap. Inside the hole is completely filled with water which is rising rapidly to spill out onto the ground. She steps to the edge. Looking down, she is relieved to see that there is no body floating underneath. The workman must have gone for help.

Something nudges her foot. It is a small wooden box which has been dislodged and floated to the surface. It is very old and as she picks it up the wood crumbles in her hands. Inside there is an ancient looking crown.

Withers is out of the cell and back at his house, brooding.

He phones up his superior, Crosby, and tells him he has bad news. "I found a supermarket in Brixton actively campaigning against milk! They had posters up advertising soya substitute saying 'Don't take risks with your health, drink soya milk instead.' When I remonstrated with the manager he threatened to frame me on a shoplifting charge."

"Did he?" says Crosby. "We'll see about that. Come and see me in the office tomorrow and we'll work out some method of dealing with him. Soya milk?"

"That's right."

"We'll fix that as well."

I'm walking down the hill to meet Pamela Patterson.

My legs refuse to work properly, it takes fierce concentration to put one in front of the other and this means that direction has to take a back seat. I'm walking back and forwards across the road and keep turning in the wrong direction, sometimes I try to take two steps with the same leg and end up stranded hopelessly, not knowing what to do next. The old couple wave at me from their balcony and I gibber briefly in their direction before setting off again, my motor control seems to have entirely deserted me and I think I'll never even get there alive.

Eventually, I reach the pub where I have to meet her, I'm early and I stand outside for a while. I'd never make it inside at all but someone comes along and brushes past me through the door. This knocks me off balance and I fall through after him. People sitting inside give me disparaging looks, drunk already, they think as I make a few involuntary circuits of the room before making it to the bar.

Give me an orange juice, I say, then skulk over to a quiet corner to wait.

Wu and Cheng have another appointment tonight in the arcade.

Wu is meditating in preparation.

Cheng is willing his working day to pass so he can get home to practice, he's already the world's finest exponent of Kill Another One but he's not taking any risks. He knows that there will be a big crowd of his supporters there tonight and he does not intend to disappoint them. Also he knows that Wu's supporters will be hoping that tonight things will be different and he is eager to show them the futility of supporting that unpleasant meditating fraud.

Poor old Wu, he laughs as he waits at the traffic lights, I wonder if he'll dare show his face?

Pamela Patterson enters the pub.

I know immediately that it is her because she is clutching a bag with comic-shaped items inside. I examine her to see if I can spot her weapon but I can't, I expect it's hidden in a shoulder holster or something.

She sees me and comes over, she asks me if I'm the person who's interested in buying comics and sits down beside me.

What a fiend, I think, sitting brazenly beside me and smiling and all the time just waiting for the right opportunity to put a bullet between my eyes. She looks very normal and not at all like a hired killer, I suppose that is the best way to be.

"Here is a rare set of *Avengers*," she says, placing Nos. 3 to 12 on the table. Despite the extreme gravity of my situation I'm impressed. I wonder if I can take her by surprise and make off with the comics as well as killing her.

She is acting her part well. She pretends an impressive knowledge of the subject and tries to engage me in a discussion on early Marvel artwork and I try to respond in a natural manner, I can't afford to let her know that I know her real mission. She certainly has done her homework thoroughly, I wonder if she learns this much about all her victims' interests?

While I'm trying to act like a normal human being I'm wound up so tight I can hardly breathe, my lungs seem to be going in opposite directions to each other, my blood is pumping round in such a manner that I feel I must be visibly vibrating.

She starts to discuss prices, what an act, but I say I don't like sitting in this pub very much, how about moving to a café that's just round the corner.

Muriel walks home carrying the crown in her bag.

Since the workman hadn't seemed interested in the ancient artefact when she mentioned it to him she figures that she had better take it to keep it safe. In the morning she can take it to a museum or something but right now she has to hurry to work. She is a nurse at a hospital and she works long hours because they are short-staffed. She wonders how the patient is who is being treated in the stationery store. He is suffering from tetanus plus a mystery disease and the stationery store is not an ideal place to keep him but there is no room anywhere else.

Although she is no expert on ancient relics, she knows that the crown she has found is extremely old and most probably valuable. She does not suppose that it will bring any financial benefit to her, being state property or something, but she does not want any harm to befall it before it is in the hands of an expert.

As she carries it she can feel a slight tingle in the tips of her fingers.

We're walking round the corner into an alleyway that leads to the café.

This is it, I act now or she's gonna shoot me. She raises her bag and I imagine that I've got about one second left.

Without warning I hit her as hard as I can. She slams into the wall without crying and I hit her again. She falls to the ground and lies still. I look round wildly for all the witnesses I expect to see running up but the alley is still quiet. She lies there not being dead and I don't know what to do. If I had a gun I guess I would shoot her, I mean, she was going to kill me for money, but I can't just beat this stranger to death.

So I search her. I'm hoping to find some evidence to tie the Milk Marketing Board in with an attempt on my life as I figure that with such a piece of evidence I could force them to lay off me. But I don't find anything. And slim chance as this was, it was about the best hope for me I could think of. I'm tempted to take the comics but I resist it and flee.

I'm running along, the motor control circuits seem to be working quite well now, I'm wondering what hired killers generally do when somebody beats them up. It crosses my mind to rush into the police station but I can imagine their reaction—officer, there's a woman lying unconscious in an alley out there, I had to do it, she was pretending to sell me comics but really she was a hired killer sent by the Milk Marketing Board—so I decide against it. I'm too scared to go home though, so I make for Fran and Julie's.

As I reach the path I trip and beat on their door with my head. My body picks this moment to give up entirely and when Julie opens the door I can only lie there looking pathetic, I try to get my mouth to work but it is out in sympathy with the rest of me.

"Why do you keep knocking on our door with your head?" asks Julie. She helps me inside.

"Would you like to swap a loaf of bread for some sulphate?" she asks as I slump onto a chair.

The Chinese man has finished his work for the day and now he is getting ready to spend the evening in his nightclub.

The prospect fills him with misery, these rich morons wandering round with their stupid smiles and stupid clothes and suntans, aged businessmen vibrating feebly to the sound of pop music and paying incredible amounts of money for alcohol, all out to have fun with girls who are there to relieve them of more money.

When he first saw the club he was under the impression that it was one of these cynical places for ripping off foreign businessmen but he learned to his surprise that no, it was serious, they like it like this, middle-aged lords mixing with tax-exile pop stars with much money and no imagination and film stars who sometimes even got their photos taken as they enter and leave the club, which is mentioned often in tabloid society pages and even there they seem to treat it seriously as a place to go if you are rich and want to be seen having a good time.

June goes back to Brixton.

She seems to be spending a lot of her time there these days. She hopes that she does not run into the man she slept with but if she does she has no doubt she can cope. She takes the comics she has bought as a way of finding her target.

Today she has hired a car because although she likes travelling on buses they are just not reliable enough to make your getaway in. She drives down and finds her way to the multi-storey car park where she parks and checks in her bag for her gun and her pile of comics.

She is slightly disguised though her disguise consists only of covering her hair with a hat and wearing a little make-up. She finds the second-hand bookshop she is looking for and asks the man behind the counter if he is interested in buying her comics. She knows that he will not be because they are too valuable for his shop.

"I'm in rather a hurry to sell them. I once met a comic collector called Alby who lived in this area," she says glibly. "Would you know him by any chance?"

"Well that's funny, you're the second girl who's asked that in the last couple of days. Was a bloke in here with his phone number, he give it to her."

"Do you know his phone number?"

"No, but I know where he lives."

"Could you give me the address?"

"Give you mine if you like. No? Oh well, I'll tell you anyway."

Because she is a well trained professional with a job to do June does not react to this except to smile at him, though given the choice she would rather shoot him. He tells her the address and June says thank you and leaves the shop.

Stacey is close to death.

The mystery illness has him in its grip and he is starting to sink, he rarely wakes and when he does he lacks the strength to mumble. The doctors look at him but they don't really know what to do, well what can you do with a mystery illness that refuses to respond to treatment?

Muriel arrives at work. On her rounds she looks in on Stacey and though there is nothing she can do for him she touches his hand out of sympathy, she is such a nice nurse that she is not even afraid of catching his mystery illness.

Immediately she touches his hand he wakes up. He sits up and smiles.

"Jesus I'm hungry," he says. "Where am I?"

As Wu nears the arcade he is approached by a young boy of about fifteen. Wu recognises him as someone he has spoken to and smiles at him. The boy is one of the young prostitutes who work in the arcade.

He says hello to Wu and tells him that he's sorry he lost last night and he hopes that tonight will go better.

"If I'm not doing some business I'll come and support you."

Wu thanks him and as the boy goes off in search of business the incident is repeated almost immediately.

As Wu draws nearer to the arcade he is greeted by more and more people who all sympathise with his defeat and wish him well for the next contest. They are all sure he can do better tonight and they all promise to come and support him.

When he reaches the arcade he finds that Cheng and his followers are already there, he can feel an unpleasant aura rising from their midst. But he is determined not to be drawn into their bad feelings so when Cheng gives him his usual poisonous greeting he smiles at him with as much sincerity as he can muster, which is quite a lot more than most people would manage in the circumstances, and walks to his machine. The watching crowd is enormous and the manager of the arcade has set their machines upon a platform so that more people can see. He has also, unknown to either player, charged an admission fee to the spectators.

Everyone is buoyant in Big Value, the entire staff is pleased that the manager is happy because now perhaps he won't moan at them as much.

Fucking hell, the cashiers sometimes say, why does he have to moan all the fucking time? They have all heard the news about the apprehension of the international shoplifting gang, the biggest story since the start of the anti-milk campaign according to the reporter from the local newspaper who came round to interview the manager and the security guard. The reporter asked questions and leered at the girls while the photographer who accompanied him took the occasional picture and also leered at the girls.

The manager does not, however, know that the dirty tricks department of the Milk Marketing Board is about to go to work on him and stands happily beside the sign that encourages people to drink soya milk substitute while he has his photo taken again, yes, we at Big Value are in the forefront of the campaign for the nation's health as well as being diligent in the detection and prevention of crime.

I'm recovering slowly though far from completely at Fran and Julie's. They ask me what's wrong but when I tell them about the person trying to kill me they seem not to believe me, in fact they lose interest altogether, bastards, it's bad enough having half of Britain gunning for me without the other half thinking I'm making it up and where does a person go to get some sympathy these days anyway?

But I'm really not feeling too good and something in my demeanour, possibly my mask of abject terror, must penetrate their thick skins eventually because they do at last recognise that I'm not in the best of spirits. They offer me some food but I'm too tense to eat and when they ask how the hamster is my eyes go misty, I thought I'd never see him again.

I'm scared to go home. I can't stay here because Fran and Julie don't allow men to spend the night under their roof, not even me. Or especially me for all I know. In fact I can't think where I can stay the night, everyone hates me too much to put me up, swine, see if you get any more sulphate off me.

I ask them if they will escort me home because I'm too scared to go alone and they think this is pretty funny but they agree, provided I give them some drugs when we get there.

"Do you want this loaf?" asks Julie.

Wu and Cheng start to play.

June knocks on the door and nothing happens.

If there is no one in she'll just have to come back tomorrow, it's not as if her employers gave her a time limit, though presumably at some stage they will get tired of waiting and start making noises, haven't you killed him yet what's keeping you, we thought he would be lying on a slab by now?

Still, there is no one home and June is not going to wait around for people to see her and memorise her face outside her intended victim's door, nor is she going to put herself in the potentially dangerous position of trying to hide somewhere nearby, better to just come back tomorrow and try again, knock on the door, he answers, splat, she fires her silenced automatic a few times, he falls backwards dead in the hall and she shuts the door and leaves, nothing to it really, especially as the front door is in a staircase in a block of flats and is visible only from the neighbouring flat.

She walks back down to her car and drives home to spend the night in solitude. Right now she is happy at the prospect.

The doctors come and look at Stacey. He is sitting up demanding food. They have no idea why he should suddenly have got better and they are a little put out, they wonder if he was faking it all along and just pretending to be in a coma.

"Were you pretending to be in a coma?" demands one of them.

Stacey looks hurt. "Of course not." He looks down at his arms and chest, at the wires and tubes which link him with various machines around the bed. "I couldn't have fooled all these machines could I?"

The doctor is not convinced. Some people have a high degree of skill in imitating illness and although he's never actually heard of anyone who could simulate brain death thus fooling the encephalograph, there is always a first time.

"Why am I in the stationery store?"

Stacey doesn't get an answer.

"What's wrong with me?"

No reply.

He considers asking the doctor if he is hard of hearing but thinks better of it, he does not want to annoy the doctor while he is in his power, which makes him think that the sooner he is out of the hospital the happier he will be, well I guess I'll be going now so if you could just take these tubes off and maybe give me a bite to eat?

"You can't go yet we have to observe you some more, nobody recovers from a mystery illness in this hospital without us knowing all about it."

Muriel comes in and says hello to Stacey and tells him she's glad he is better.

"At least somebody is," says Stacey gloomily.

We reach my flat and I put the kettle on while Fran and Julie go to talk to the hamster.

He is always pleased to see them. Look what I've got for you, says Fran, and gives him a biscuit, he takes it enthusiastically and stuffs it into the vast pouches on either side of his mouth, you wouldn't believe how much this hamster can put into these pouches, something to do with another dimension, I think.

They continue talking while I make some tea and feel relieved that no one killed me as I came up the stairs and the door did not explode as I opened it, it has struck me recently that this hitwoman might be an all round weapons expert capable of killing me without even coming near me, she might booby trap the house or fire a homing missile at me or any number of things.

I try to put such thoughts out of my head and concentrate on making tea. Generally I make a pretty mean cup of tea as anyone who knows me will freely admit, a hopeless case, yes, but he does make good tea.

Somehow my problems seem far from solved. What if that person comes after me again? What if the Milk Marketing Board decides I still have to go, low profile or not? They might even hire another killer. What about this Chinese man who's leading his Triad against me? What about the way it always rains on me when I go out so my hair looks stupid? What about the way the wind always blows it about even if I've spent more than an hour in front of a mirror getting it just right? What about these black lines under my eyes that won't go away? I heard a doctor on a phone-in on the radio giving health advice and I phoned up but the person answering the calls, some lackey, said they had too many important calls about cancer and things to have time to ask the doctor about lines under someone's eyes, so what makes you think that cancer is more important than black lines under my eyes, I began to ask him, but he cut me off, bastard. What about my dry skin? What about the noise from the big trucks that deliberately change gear outside my window? What about that time last week when that man in the shop tried to short change me?

I feel depressed about how hard life is.

Professor Wing is in a state of deep, profound misery.

All his life he has read books on ancient British history. No one knows more about the subject than he does. But when he had a chance to actually find a relic of these times by himself, he blew it. He does not think that he can go back to the site now, certainly not in his workman's disguise, he would be found out and apprehended for sure.

Perhaps after the road is repaired he can announce his findings to the world in the usual way. Then an official search party can dig up the road and find the crown and he will still receive credit. He wishes he had done that in the first place.

He looks down at his feet, still wet from today's unfortunate experience. He has not yet dried them. This is a sort of subconscious penance.

He wonders if he should try to return the stolen clothes and equipment to the council or if he should just dump them somewhere. He can't decide. Weary, he turns on the radio to listen to some classical music, he likes classical music. He catches a newsflash, divers still occupying oil rig while bailiffs battle through high seas to serve writ requiring them to leave. The report reminds him of several moments in English history. More or less everything reminds him of several moments in English history.

Cheng has won the first game by a narrow margin and the second has just begun.

Once, a long time ago, two friends played for fun in the arcade across the street from the flat they shared in Soho, the games became more closely fought as they both acquired skill, slowly they became rivals though neither of them noticed it happening, their skill attracted the attention of a few people who hung around the arcade and their games began to win an audience, as they became better and better more and more people began to watch, they would stand quietly around in small groups making friendly comments in between rounds, the rivalry increased and Cheng began to dislike Wu, he moved out of the flat on some pretext or other and almost immediately they were enemies, their communication dropped to the point of arranging where and when to meet and all the time more and more people were coming to watch them and when they played the crowd was no longer quiet or friendly but loud, aggressive, and hostile.

Cheng wins the second game. Wu's supporters start to look sad. It looks as if last night's proceedings are going to be repeated.

It's funny the way that lonely people hanging round with nothing much to do and no one much to talk to have taken naturally to Wu. They shout encouragement to him but he cannot hear them in his trance.

The crown that Muriel found has magic powers. They only work in the right hands. Because Muriel is psychic she has involuntarily picked up these powers. So when she touched Stacey and wished he would get better, he immediately recovered.

In the course of her duties as a nurse she is, of course, touching patients all the time. The crown has wakened her own latent powers as well as giving her some of its own, and all the patients she touches instantly start to heal. This leads to many pleased patients but insanely suspicious doctors driven mad by the sudden epidemic of good health that is sweeping their hospital.

Eventually Muriel will notice some correlation between events and realise that she has healing powers. She will go on to become a famous healer.

This is all some time in the future, however, and right now she is hurrying round the hospital trying to get all of her work done in some satisfactory manner, along with almost everyone else in the hospital she is run off her feet and never has time to do everything she should.

They are permanently short-staffed. If times are particularly hard due to staff sickness then everyone seems to work almost twenty-four hours a day. They quickly fall into a trance-like state, walking the corridors half asleep and trying to remember where they are going.

Fran and Julie hang around my house for a while listening to records and drinking tea.

"Will you come and visit me tomorrow to make sure I'm still alive?"

Julie says that her kung fu teacher is coming round to visit them tomorrow.

I've never met their kung fu teacher, some brute I expect, well bring her up, I say, please come and see if I'm alive, if I die you won't have anyone to bring you speed.

This argument carries considerable weight and they say all right, they may call up if they've got time, well thanks, I think, don't put yourself out, I mean it's only a matter of my life. But I don't labour the point.

They have brought some stolen food to my flat and they leave it with me because when evening rolls around they really can't be bothered to think of things like eating. I give them the sulphate I promised them, a large amount.

After they've gone I barricade the door and sit down to worry. I make sure I'm not in view through any of the windows, though you can't actually see through any of the windows in my flat as they are so dirty it's hard to tell where the wall ends and the glass begins, but anyway I'm not taking any chances.

I think again about how I can sell my comics and raise money but I got no fresh thoughts. I'd ask Happy if he has any bright new notions but he has gone to sleep to digest his biscuit and I don't like to disturb him, I expect he's having a rest before going out tonight.

I have a nagging pain in my lungs and if there is one place where a pain is going to worry you an awful lot it's in your lungs. I immediately think of the most painless way to kill myself in case it's lung cancer, I don't want to suffer through that, the very thought makes me sweat. I dig around the area with my fingers trying to convince myself that it is just a muscular pain but it's no use, there is definitely something wrong with my lungs. I'm scared to cough in case I bring up some blood, I hurry to a mirror to see how I look, it is hard to get a good impression of the state of your lungs from a mirror but perhaps it might show in my eyes or something.

My eyes are looking pretty bad.

Cheng has won the third game in convincing fashion and now leads by three games to nil. Cheng's supporters are laughing and singing songs while deep gloom spreads in the opposite camp.

The manager of Big Value is spending his lunch hour on the phone to Pinelog Limited, finding out more details of their Swedish-style Chalet Pools. He considers placing a firm order but restrains himself, you never know, some malicious executive high up in the company might still want to withhold his bonus.

After Fran and Julie leave Alby's flat they return home to take some speed.

They wonder about Alby's bizarre fears and fantasies, he has not quite been himself since that business over milk and thinks that the entire world is out to get him.

"What he needs is more drugs."

One day I have a hard time getting home from a delivery.

I'm on a bus and we get close to Brixton. The bus stops behind a big traffic jam and I'm upstairs looking round when I see a blind man across the street, he has a big white stick and he wants to cross the road.

There are two people with him, a tall person and a small one, I don't know whether they are friends or strangers, but instead of walking up to the traffic lights thirty yards up the road, they're waiting for a break in the traffic through which they can hurry across. On the other side of the bus, the side I can't see, there is shouting. I'm scared the blind man is going to die, his companions are shuffling him on and off the road waiting for their chance to cross, eventually there's a gap in the traffic and they hurry across, they're almost there and I'm hoping they made it when the shouting on the other side gets louder and a voice shouts "Put that knife away!" For fuck's sake, I think, and shrink into my newspaper. What's going on and will it leave me alone?

The bus moves off. I don't see if the blind man made it. Whoever is waving a knife around doesn't leap on and stab me as I feared. One more lucky escape.

Across the aisle from me is a very fat youth, he's talking to two girls. He is a crazed extrovert and in between his words he keeps bursting into song, an old soul number called "What a Night." They get off the bus before I do, this guy is really fat, I look out when he is travelling on up the pavement, he smacks a fist into the palm of his hand then punches the air and bursts into song again, "Get down on it!" he sings, then turns back to his conversation. He sings terribly.

I get off the bus when it is as close to my house as it goes. I'm walking up the road when I see two small children playing in the road, well not exactly playing, they are putting a bottle out for cars to burst their tyres on. I like to see car tyres burst as much as the next person but I realise that more than likely the car will leave the road at high velocity and hit possibly the children and certainly me so I cross the road and pick up the bottle. I glare at the kids to put them off and call them stupid bastards and toss the bottle casually over the fence beside the pavement, but I toss it too casually and it hits the top and bursts all over me. The children have hysterics. I'm going to whap them a good one across the face but they run away too quick.

I walk away embarrassed and behind me they are still laughing.

After all these terrible experiences I hurry home to hide and sulk.

I'm looking at my lungs in the mirror. The pain seems to be spreading.

It's becoming more and more difficult to breathe, I go and take some vitamin C in one last desperate effort and it seems to help, you can cure a lot of things with vitamin C, you know, I'm told that vitamin E helps retard aging and in consequence I more or less live on the stuff, when I go into the health food store these days they put a couple of boxes on the counter in readiness.

Fran and Julie have gone and I'm on my own, I've made them promise to look in on me tomorrow and I think I'll be all right till then. I'm not sure how much to worry in the meantime. I put Captain Sinbad on the record player, I always feel that record player is not a very hip thing to call it but it's the way I was brought up.

I look at the kitchen floor and it's thick with dirt and chips and old lettuce leaves, well it gives the place a friendly atmosphere, I get a pan out to boil some water for tea, not long ago I melted the kettle due to being distracted by the drum machine and I haven't been able to buy another one since, it's not so easy to buy a new kettle, you know, there's a lot of different kinds to choose from, I want some high technology model but they cost an awful lot so I suppose I'll end up with some cheap utility thing.

Wu is losing five games to nothing and his supporters are looking dejected and embarrassed. Cheng has reached dazzling new peaks of skill. No one has ever played Kill Another One like this before.

After game number five they halt, every five games they have a break. Cheng talks with his fans, Wu stays quiet. Among the crowd are some police officers who patrol the Soho area. They support Cheng. The police aren't very big on meditation.

June lies on her bed.

She has checked her gun and it is in good working order. Tomorrow she is going back to Brixton to kill Alby.

I'm lying around the flat waiting for tomorrow to appear.

I never could spell tomorrow, along with address it's one of the worst words in the language and probably no one can spell it correctly.

I'm looking at a magazine I picked up from the ground outside the estate. Inside it are lots of articles which are meant to be funny but they may as well be written in a foreign language for all the humour I can see in them, also there is an advert for a book competition, the Sinclair Prize or something like that, send in your socially aware book, it says, you fucking wankers, I think, advertising for socially aware books in this glossy upmarket humour magazine, just what would you know about social awareness and what exactly do you mean anyway, I suppose it means something they can discuss on arts programmes on television without getting embarrassed.

I throw the magazine out of the window and read some comics.

The next day is almost here, I wonder what I'll do with it when it comes.

Stacey is still forcibly confined to bed in the hospital, he had harboured an illusion that there was some voluntary element to being in the hospital but apparently not, he needn't think they're going to let him out just because he feels better.

But he does sneak out of bed in between doctors' visits and he sees a new patient being brought in, he is surprised to recognise her, it's Pamela Patterson, the young woman he met in the second-hand book shop, the one he'd given Alby's phone number to. She looks like she's been beaten up. She was found like this in an alley in Brixton, a nurse tells him.

"The police say a gang of blacks done it."

Pamela is clutching a bag of comics.

June gets into the car and heads out. She is driving down to complete her assignment. She thinks about the lack of female philosophers, or rather the lack of published ones.

The Chinese man is suffering at his nightclub.

He smiles at the customers and as they stumble round making as much noise as is humanly possible he thinks are these people for real? A man approaches him, the man thinks you might own this place but you're just a Chinaman and I'm English and what's more I'm a lord so the question of who is better just doesn't arise.

He speaks to the lord in a friendly sort of way. The Chinese man supposes that when he meets the woman he's going to marry then she will have relatives like these nightclubbers, seeing as she will be a member of the aristocracy in some capacity, still he won't have to socialise with them too much in nightclubs, what he has in mind is more along the lines of garden parties in large marquees, dinners in the stately home, he has the money so surely others can provide some refinement. Looking around him, he's not so sure.

The woman who teaches Julie kung fu is called Chi. She was lucky to escape from Burma after the warlord she served was killed in a large-scale gun battle. As one of his bodyguards she fought loyally before being forced to flee when the situation degenerated into hopelessness and the warlord was killed. As far as she knows she is the only member of the bodyguard to have escaped, she fled through Cambodia and Vietnam in the company of another employee of the warlord.

Things actually looked quite bright for a while because as they fled they managed to take with them a large quantity of gold from the camp. But on the way out of Vietnam her companion tricked her and left her stranded. Alone and penniless she had a hard time leaving the country and was several times fortunate to escape with her life.

Now she is content. Generally she finds it better teaching kung fu in Brixton than acting as an armed bodyguard in Burma, much less dangerous if not as exciting.

Muriel sits at home and examines the crown. It is of simple design, little more than a plain circlet of gold with some runes engraved, as she touches it she feels a tingling sensation.

Now that she has it she is not too sure what to do with it. What do you do with ancient archaeological treasures that float up to the surface of a hole in the road in an old wooden box? She supposes that she should take it to an expert somewhere.

She places it back in its crumbled box and puts it in a cupboard before going to bed.

She is tired, she always is, she works hard.

A team of official council roadwork troubleshooters are examining the mysterious flooded hole in the road.

How, they wonder, did this unofficial hole come to be here? The council has no records of anyone being sent here, no record of any work being needed in this area. The matter is deeply perplexing and the more they think about it the more puzzling it becomes until it begins to take on Bermuda Triangle proportions.

Newspaper men are hot on the story. MYSTERIOUS HOLE CAUSES FLOOD IN BRIXTON, WAS IT A METEOR? "Scientists and council repairmen were today completely baffled by the appearance of a strange new hole in the pavement in south London."

I lie awake in bed worrying about things in general, my blood doesn't feel very good and I think I might have contracted AIDS.

It's hard getting a blood test even if you are almost certainly suffering from some appalling killer disease, go down to the hospital and ask them in a reasonable manner to put medical science to work on your behalf and give your blood a quick scan while you wait and they will tell you to go to hell. Bastards.

One time in desperation I went to give blood, reasoning that if there was anything wrong with it then they would pick it up as presumably they don't just pump it untested into the bodies of the sick, not that I believe the blood transfusion service is really as altruistic as they pretend, in fact I expect they take the blood you give them and sell it to the USA.

Giving blood wasn't too terrible and made me feel brave and helpful to others, it didn't hurt but you have to lie on a table for about half an hour while it seeps out of your arm, I kinda imagined they'd just stick a hole in your vein and a pint of blood would flow out in about twenty seconds but for some reason it takes a long time. It flows out into a transparent bag which you can look at if you're feeling morbid. What if there was a fire and everyone fled leaving you there, flat out with a tube in your arm?

But after giving blood and lying down to rest I go over to get my cup of tea as promised and the nurse refuses to give me one, well for fuck's sake do you think I'd have given blood if I had thought I wasn't even going to get a cup of tea at the end of it? She spins me some pathetic story about is it the first time, well you can't have no tea, something to do with body temperatures, all she'll give me is orange juice and that is just not the same.

They do have biscuits and I eat as many as I possibly can but they don't give me any iron tablets either, a shoddy way to treat the nation's heroes if you ask me.

The Chinese man is hiding in his office at the nightclub. He is thinking about putting a personal ad in a magazine and wonders how to phrase it. "Good looking rich oriental drug financier seeks aristocratic wife." No, that doesn't seem quite right. He'll have to work on it a bit.

Wu rallies slightly and wins a game. He is well into his altered meditative state and his consciousness drifts out of his body and into the machine in front of him. As the machine, he looks out and plays his body.

The packed audience generates heat and the arcade becomes stuffy, full of noise and cigarette smoke. This is a good environment for playing video games and Cheng revels in it, taking strength from the unhealthy air.

Fran and Julie go down to a local pub with enough money for one and a half drinks but plenty of confidence that they can rustle up some more, this is a friendly place and they know many people who may come in and even if almost all of these people are broke there is bound to be someone with some money to spare and if there turns out not to be they will survive, they have taken enough sulphate to levitate a rhinoceros so they won't be completely bored.

The pub they go to in Brixton is tolerable as pubs go, frequented by people largely concerned with dyeing their hair the correct shade and getting through life without starving to death before the next giro arrives from the social security, the social security are well known enemies of society populated by senior officers who take physical pleasure in watching people starve, yes, we've sent your money they will say over the phone when in reality they have lost the papers relating to your claim, have no idea where they are and really couldn't give a fuck.

The speed is taking effect by the time they reach the pub and they wander in happily and spend all their money on one and a half drinks which they share, it takes them several seconds to drink them and they look round enthusiastically for someone to buy them some more. Julie ruffles her hands through the considerable volume of her rainbow hair then does the same over Fran's cropped head.

Well who can we get a drink off, they say to each other, how about that woman over there, didn't we meet her one time?

I wake up with the quilt over my head.

I take this as an omen and resolve not to get out of bed today. I lie for a while in much comfort, waking up without actually having to get out of bed is one of the things I most enjoy, always providing I don't wake up feeling ill.

So I'm lying there with no intention of moving in the forseeable future when there is a knock on the door.

Jesus who is calling at this time in the morning, I put my arm out of the bed and grope around feebly for my watch, by a near miracle it is close by and I see that it is a quarter past eleven, disgraceful to disturb someone at a quarter past eleven, I think, I don't want to get up and besides I'm still scared of knocks on the door because it might be Pamela Patterson or it might be that oriental person who is pursuing me.

So I decide not to answer it but when there is a further rap on the door I remember that I've asked Fran and Julie up today and that they are going to be with Julie's kung fu teacher who is no doubt a health fanatic given to tramping the streets before the break of dawn. So I stumble up and look in the mirror, find some trousers on the floor and get into them, look in the mirror again, try and get my hair into place, fasten the trousers, look in the mirror, and head for the front door.

I press my eye to the spyhole and I'm astonished to see June, the person I slept with after that gig the other night, well how about that, she must have really liked me to have found out where I live and come down to visit me.

I open the door enthusiastically and she pulls a gun out of her pocket and points it at my chest.

Crosby and Withers are in conference at Milk Headquarters.

Alby Starvation is still alive, notes Crosby with displeasure.

"Well it couldn't really be helped," Withers tells him. "The agency wasn't to know that the person they sent would be converted before he arrived."

"What's happened to him?"

"He's still handing out leaflets. And before the next hitperson could reach Mr Starvation he got a mysterious tip-off from somewhere and went underground. But he should be dead any day now."

"Good." says Crosby. "Now, about that branch of Big Value that's trying to frame you. We can't have major chain stores pushing soya milk, it's just not on. Our objective must be to disgrace the manager and blacken this product, shouldn't be too hard on either count, he's probably a crook anyway. And this soya milk probably tastes foul, soya everything else does."

They get down to discussing details. After they have completed their plan Withers takes the rest of the day off. He goes to the offices of the Institute of Directors and calls in at a room on the ground floor. There is a sign on the door, it reads DEPARTMENT FOR NULLIFYING CRIMINAL PROCEEDINGS.

The manager of Big Value is out celebrating with his wife.

They are eating in a restaurant and afterwards they are going on to a nightclub, the manager's wife is looking forward to this because the number of times she goes out is not very large. The meal costs a vast amount of money. She finds it hard to believe that people can charge so much for food, no matter what they've done to it. Still, this is small potatoes to a man with a sales bonus on the way so she tries not to resent the expense, just give me this much money to spend during the day and I wouldn't be so bored, she thinks.

What is more, she worries that she will be too old for the nightclub but her husband assures her that he knows just the place, somewhere in Soho that his directors go to when they are having fun.

Spinach is just as bad as lettuce, you get it and put it in a pot and boil it for a while and when it's done you look at it and think for God's sake is this some sort of joke, I mean surely no one eats this sort of thing for pleasure? It lies there looking like some rare green fungus, they tell me it's packed full of iron but personally I would rather chew on the cutlery.

When I get up my nerve I find it doesn't taste quite as bad as it looks but that is not saying much. I try palming it off on the hamster but he's not having any of it, I'm healthy enough already, he says.

There is some deep relationship between the unpleasantness of food and its nutritional value but I'm afraid it's beyond my mental capacity to work it out. It seems like someone's trying to teach me a lesson, if you're going to get through life Alby, you just got to eat the odd bit of spinach now and then.

Fran and Julie are hopelessly wrecked.

They leave the pub happily at closing time and head for the rat-infested hole round the corner where there will be some sort of gig on, a kindly friend leads them there and points them through the door, they don't have any money but they know the man on the door and he lets them in because if he didn't he knows they would only cause trouble.

"Not a bad evening so far," says Julie to Fran.

Fran mumbles agreement.

I don't understand this development in the proceedings. Why is this person pointing a gun at me? Did I do something wrong in bed? Surely it couldn't have been that unpleasant for her.

Perhaps she wants her army trousers back, well she only has to ask. I try to say something but I can't manage it. I notice that June is looking a bit puzzled.

"Are you Alby Starvation?" she asks.

I nod.

"I'm here to kill you," she says. "I'm working for the Milk Marketing Board."

I find this difficult to take in and I sag from the knees.

She comes in and closes the door behind her, still pointing the gun at my chest.

June knocks on the door, nothing happens, she knocks again, after a while she hears footsteps. When the door opens she takes out her gun, points it, and is on the verge of squeezing the trigger when to her astonishment she realises that the person on the receiving end is none other than the man she slept with just the other night.

"Are you Alby Starvation?" she asks, and he says he is and looks scared.

June can't believe it. She walks forward a few paces and closes the door behind her. She doesn't know quite what to do, nothing like this has ever happened before, killing someone you know doesn't seem quite the same as killing someone you've never met and the fact that she has slept with this person makes things even stranger.

She would like to just shoot and get it over with and she reckons that this is probably the best policy but somehow she can't quite bring herself to do it.

I find it hard to take in this development. How many killers has the Milk Marketing Board hired?

"But you're not Pamela Patterson," I say.

She doesn't reply, it's hard getting this conversation going with the gun pointing at my chest. This is the person I just slept with. It's too horrible to contemplate. Who was that Pamela Patterson person? Why did she pretend she was a hired killer out to get me? But I don't have time to think about it because it may be my imagination or it may be my hyperdeveloped sense of self-preservation but it seems to me that June's finger is tightening on the trigger.

"Don't kill me," I whine, for want of anything better.

"I'm afraid I have to, I've got a contract."

"But we slept together just the other night. We like each other."

"One doesn't naturally follow from the other."

"But even so, you surely can't kill me?"

I'm sure there must be a better line of argument but for the moment it eludes me. I'll have to stick to whining. How could this possibly happen? Has someone been planning it all? Maybe she knew who I was all the time and wanted to sleep with me before killing me for some perverted reason, the whole world is made up of freaks and it wouldn't surprise me if hired killers had some peculiarly unpleasant facets to their personalities. My fear is making me pour with sweat.

"You seemed lonely the other night and I was friendly to you, surely you don't want to kill me?" This sounds better, I think.

I can feel blood evaporating in my veins.

June considers what Alby says.

From a professional point of view, she doesn't really have sufficient reason not to kill him, and if she deliberately refuses to carry out the contract then her agency will discharge her from their employment and she won't get any more contracts and her source of income will be gone. Normally the job would have been done by now, she would have fired before her victim had a chance to speak. Usually her victims do not even see her. Alby's talking makes him seem like a real person and this puts her off.

She doesn't know what to do.

The manager of Big Value and his wife are dancing in the nightclub that is partly owned by the Chinese man. She thinks it is the worst place she has ever been in her life. Isn't it time to go home yet?

The crown that Muriel found is a powerful icon.

The magician who used it in his neighbourhood war back in the time of Ethelred the Unready originally located it in Egypt, where it was old even then, and brought it back to Britain after trading with its owner. Not many British people made it to Egypt in those days and he was quite well received there as a curiosity. They could tell he was an evil magician but he wasn't powerful enough to do them any harm, in Egypt they had been practising magic since time immemorial. But he brought them some plants from the north that they would have had difficulty getting their hands on otherwise and also a chip off a meteor so they gave him the crown he wanted and told him to give their best wishes to everyone in Britain.

He used the crown to defeat his neighbour, also a magician but not one normally disposed to harming others. He might have gone much further and conquered the entire country but his interests suddenly changed and he immersed himself in science and mathematics rather than magic.

So he put the crown away in a drawer and began making calculations about the rotation of the planets and things like that, things he had glimpsed in Egypt.

One time I lost a toy robot in a biscuit barrel on a bus.

My heart is rended. They are both presents, it is a brilliant robot and I am hurrying home to play with it, I nip into the biscuit shop to put some biscuits in my new biscuit barrel and get on a bus, I plan to spend the day eating biscuits and playing with the robot. But I leave it on the bus.

It is a dreadful experience and I am really upset to think of this robot being kidnapped and taken home by some stranger. I go next day to the London Transport lost property office but they deny all knowledge of the affair.

I expect that some of their staff are in on it. When I go in asking for a toy robot on a biscuit barrel some people around actually start laughing. Bastards.

Poor robot.

Fran and Julie are ruined beyond description.

They've almost reached their flat but at the final corner they've forgotten the way, after a few seconds contemplating the matter they forget what they're trying to do and settle down to sit on the pavement and gurgle at the night. They could well be here for a long time but a kindly neighbour on her way back from a late night film finds them and takes them home. When they reach their squat the neighbour locates Fran's key and opens the door, goodnight, she says, as they shamble inside.

When they reach the first place large enough to lie down in they slump onto the floor and go to sleep.

Wu is pulling back. In his altered state he is starting to overtake the conscious concentration of Cheng.

Some way away at the far end of the arcade in a private office the arcade manager is counting money, one of the things he likes about owning the arcade is that he actually gets to count the money. He finds the physical presence of notes and coins immensely satisfying, he doubts if he could be happy working in computer fraud.

He runs arcades all over London. Some of them are fairly honest while others are no more than fronts for criminal enterprises. Whenever he wants to expand his criminal activities he phones up an inspector at the police station and asks for a permit, the inspector says yes, certainly you can, just a second till I get the price list.

As the arcade manager counts his money he puts a percentage on one side. This is the money for the police inspector. The inspector comes, good day, how are you, he says, they are quite friendly, no problems in the arrangement, the inspector gives the money to the constable who is with him and tells him to wait in the car while he has a drink and a chat, after a few minutes swapping news he leaves and drives on to his next pick-up spot.

The constable who is driving him is pleased to be there as he is eager to learn the trade and keen for advancement in the force.

When they arrive home from the club her husband is slightly drunk. He is muttering oblique references to international shoplifting gangs and socialist newspapers that get sold every Saturday outside his store.

"They probably poisoned the cat."

She wonders about her life, she can't quite understand how it ended up like this. It's not as if she hates her husband or even dislikes him, it's just that the totality of their existence seems to be one enormous bore. While he stumbles off to bed she stays up, sitting in the kitchen on a hard wooden chair, she feels like reading something but she can't find a book, where have all my books gone? So she looks at the walls. Why, she thinks, did we put such appalling paper on the kitchen walls? Then she remembers, they saw it in a colour supplement.

When she gets down to thinking about it there is not much about their flat that she likes. It's not that any of it is in particularly bad taste, it's just that it is fantastically dull. And why, she thinks, am I spending my life surrounded by dull wallpaper.

Oh fuck this, I mean no one goes to bed with some strange woman then finds them practically the next day brandishing a weapon on the doorstep and asking if you have any last words.

I know I won't be able to convince myself this is all a dream so I just stand and whine for a while and wonder about the girl I attacked in Brixton, I'm sorry Pamela, it was like this you see, there's this killer after me and I thought that you were her, an understandable mistake I'm sure you'll agree. Yes, I realise now that you only wanted to sell me some comics but I thought that was just a cover story. Are you still interested in selling them?

This is assuming that I am still alive after the next minute or so and right now I'm not too confident, well I don't suppose I'm ever too confident that I'll still be alive after the next minute or so but this is worse than usual.

I make the last move of a desperate man and ask June if she would like a cup of tea.

Withers has fixed things at the Department for Nullifying Criminal Proceedings at the Institute of Directors, he just shows them his membership card and tells them what offence he is charged with and where it took place and they get in touch with the police and arrange for it to be forgotten about. We look after our members, says the Institute, that's what they want us for.

Then Withers gets down to planning his revenge on the manager of Big Value in such a way as to completely ruin his career while also dealing a death blow to soya milk substitute. This should not prove to be too difficult, these things never are, his department does them all the time.

After the magician lost interest in the crown it fell into disuse. He was developing a new concept of mathematical warfare and had no further use for magical items, nonetheless he realised that others might try to steal the crown so he hid it and got his secretary to write some cryptic directions as to its whereabouts. And there it lay forgotten for centuries until by chance the directions, buried in the earthquake, were found by the professor.

When Muriel opened the box a strong wave of mystic energy washed out over the area. This energy was felt by several people attuned to such things. Some of them are now trying to discover the source of the energy.

On her day off Muriel takes the crown to a department of the university which is quite near to where she lives. She hands it over to the secretary in the history faculty who assures Muriel that she will pass it on to someone who knows about such things. The secretary thinks that Muriel is some nut who has found an old piece of metal on a scrapyard or something and gets rid of her as quickly as she can.

Stacey, completely recovered but still confined to the hospital, seeks out Pamela Patterson. He finds her lying in bed with a bandage round her head. She recognises him but does not seem too pleased to see him.

"Thanks for that phone number," she says. "Always nice to be put in touch with a violent maniac."

Stacey does not understand. "What do you mean?"

She tells him that the person whose phone number he gave her, the one who said he might be interested in buying the comics, attacked her in an alleyway. Vicious and unprovoked.

Stacey is amazed. "That doesn't sound like Alby."

"You don't say."

"Did he steal the comics?"

"No."

Stacey is puzzled. It doesn't sound like Alby to attack anyone although he could understand him being driven to violence by the sight of a comic he couldn't afford.

"Did you tell the police who done it?"

"No."

"Why not?"

"They didn't ask."

June is completely put off by being offered a cup of tea by her intended victim and gives up the task. Oh well, I can probably find another agency, she thinks, or else get a job in an office somewhere.

She puts her gun away. "All right, Alby, I don't suppose I can shoot you in view of the fact that we know each other. It's unethical to give up on a contract like this you know."

"Perhaps it would be unethical to kill someone you've slept with," says Alby, sounding relieved. "Like a doctor operating on his lover?"

They go into the kitchen, June looks round at the mess while he makes some tea, this is the sort of house you have to wipe your feet when you leave. She was amazed at first when she learned the identity of her contract but she has got over it now, these things happen in an infinite universe you know, here she is drinking tea with him now.

She doesn't mind Alby, he can be person number four on the list of people she doesn't actively dislike.

Professor Wing, utterly dispirited, arrives for work at the University. He says good morning to the departmental secretary and she says good morning, someone just brought something into the department, it looks like an old bit of metal but I had to humour her by promising to get it appraised, would you like to look at it?

She brings out the crown.

The professor takes hold of it, he recognises immediately by its shape that it could be very old. He examines the runes round the edge. As soon as he reads them he realises what it is.

He goes cold inside. As the crown could not have arrived here by chance then some external force must have entered the arena. He waits to be either struck down by a thunderbolt from God or arrested by a member of the police force.

When neither happens he manages with some difficulty to speak to the secretary. He asks her about the person who handed the crown in. He recognises the woman from the secretary's description and after a few seconds' puzzlement he realizes what must have happened. She must have gone back to the site after he left and somehow found the crown. But how had she known to bring it here? Could it have been coincidence after all?

"Did she say she would be back?" he asks.

The secretary tells him yes, she said she would try and call back some time to see if the metal band was of any importance.

Wu is now level with Cheng.

The watching crowd is spellbound at the dazzling skill being displayed by both players, Cheng sweating and swearing, Wu oblivious to the world.

Wu's consciousness has expanded so that it now overlaps with that of everyone in the hall. Through the eyes of the manager he sees the police inspector come and go. He realises that the manager is using him and Cheng to make money. He sees the screen in front of Cheng and feels his desire to win. He experiences the riveted concentration of the spectators. In harmony with the arcade, the machines and the people, Wu knows that he can win.

Chi, fresh from her early morning exercise, knocks on the door of the squat that Fran and Julie live in. They have invited her round for the day but there is no reply so she knocks again. To her surprise the door swings open. Slightly worried in case anything is wrong, she enters the building.

As she turns the first corner in the long gloomy hall she walks straight into the prostrate body of Fran, which is lying in a huddle on top of Julie. Chi is alarmed, but relieved when the body moans and turns over, at least they aren't dead, she prods Fran with her toe which produces another moan. Chi sees that they have not been attacked, shot, or poisoned but are suffering only from self-inflicted body abuse.

"Good morning, Julie!" she calls to the still unconscious figure underneath. "I have called as invited. Would you like me to make you some tea?"

Julie and Fran moan in unison.

Julie opens her eyes. "I haven't been to sleep yet. What time is it?"

"It is past midday and you did promise me lunch, but nevermind, just get up and ready and we'll go for a walk."

Fran rises with unexpected swiftness.

"Excuse me," she says. "I must just go and be sick."

Next day the manager, slightly hungover, is sitting in his office just prior to opening time. Outside in the store one of the supervisors is on the point of opening the doors to start the day's trading when she sees several large figures approaching. They knock on the glass door.

"Just a second," she calls out. "I'm just opening."

The door shatters into streaming fragments as one of the men kicks his way through it, he shoves the mangled wreckage out of the way and steps into Big Value. The others follow him.

"Good morning, miss," he says, showing her his identification card. "We're police officers. We'd like to interview the manager. Where is he?"

The supervisor is in a state of shock. "Why didn't you wait till I opened the door?" she asks, keys still clutched in hand and bits of glass in her hair.

"That's not the way we do things, darling. And we'll ask the questions. Now, where is he?"

I'm having a cup of tea with June, she has put her gun away which is some relief, I can tell you.

I'm not entirely sure what to say and conversation is a bit strained, I don't want to lead it in the wrong direction in case she changes her mind.

"How are your plants?"

"You don't like plants."

"Is the tea all right?"

"Yes."

It doesn't seem to be going too well. I'm having difficulty being my natural self with someone who, only moments ago, was all set to consign me to the netherworld. I wonder if I should mention Pamela Patterson to her but decide against it, I realise that I'm still half undressed and what's more my hair is probably a mess, excuse me while I go and get dressed, I mumble, and depart to the bedroom.

What an all-time awkward situation this is, I think while rummaging around on the floor for something to wear. She follows me through as I'm looking in the mirror.

"Why are you so vain?" she asks.

"What me? I don't think I'm very vain, what makes you say that, I was just checking to see if I looked ill, I'm a sick man you know."

She looks round and comments on the extreme disorder of the room. "I'm surprised you can find the bed."

"Well I like it this way. It makes life a challenge."

She looks at my comics, piled carefully against the walls.

"These look pretty stupid," she says.

I'm shocked. Outraged. Stupid? My comics? Stupid? She is lucky she's got that gun on her. Nobody calls Alby Starvation's comics stupid and lives to tell the tale.

Neck and neck and the last game starts. Wu has no need to worry or to hurry, his movements, though fast to those watching, are slow and careful inside. For Wu, time has slowed down.

Now that he knows he can win he finds himself in an unexpected dilemma. He has looked into the mind of Cheng and into those of his supporters and wonders now whether victory means so much to him that he wants to cause such distress to his opponents. He sees that defeat will be a shattering blow to Cheng and will cause him much misery and pain.

On the other hand his supporters are depending on him, although why they are so bound up with his success or failure is something he still does not quite understand. There is a young man standing beside him hoping desperately that he wins, yet Wu sees into his mind and knows that they have never even met. He can see the young man's extreme loneliness as he stands close and comforts himself with Wu's presence.

"Excuse me," says Julie to Fran, "but if you've finished being sick in the toilet perhaps you could let me in for a turn."

"Can't you use the sink?"

"It's still blocked."

Chi makes them some tea. After some considerable time they appear, they both look terrible.

"What did you have last night?"

Julie looks innocent. She does not want to tell her kung fu teacher about the vast amount of alcohol and illicit substances she consumes.

"Nothing, nothing at all."

"Then why are you throwing up and looking like you're going to die?"

"Something we ate?" volunteers Fran.

"Yes," says Julie. "It must have been something we ate."

"It must have been something particularly virulent to have made you both collapse in the hall like that."

"It must have affected us quickly. Salmonella can be pretty vicious when it attacks."

Wu deliberately loses the last game and in doing so gives overall victory to Cheng.

Professor Wing looks lovingly at the crown. He reads the runes blows a speck of dust from the rim, holds it up to the light.

How, he wonders, is he going to announce the find to the world? Honestly or dishonestly?

His secretary buzzes him.

"The woman who handed in the parcel is back. Do you want to see her?"

The professor does not want to see her but feels unable to refuse. What if she recognises him as the workman who was digging up the road? But perhaps she will not, after all he looks very different in a suit.

She enters the office.

"Why, it's the man who was digging up the road," she says.

While Cheng and his friends celebrate, Wu seeks out the young man who was standing beside him during the contest and tries to cheer him up. More of his fans gather round and he tries to cheer them up as well. It is a difficult task.

Although he does not normally socialise, Wu goes with his supporters to a pub close by.

Back in the kitchen I switch on the radio to fill in the gaps in our conversation.

I hear a report from a new exhibition of British natural history. Natural history means animals and plants, a strange term I have always thought. Do they have to be dead to be natural history or can they still be living or does it not matter?

The reporter and the curator are just moving on from weeds to bugs.

"Well," says the reporter, "I wouldn't like to come across something like this, you say it's found indoors?"

"Yes," replies the curator. "It's a cardinal spider, this specimen is four inches long but they do come bigger."

My skin crawls. A four-inch spider on the loose inside your home?

"Jesus'" I say. "I'd die if I found a four-inch spider in here. Why hasn't there been a national campaign to eradicate them? Shouldn't the government be doing something?"

"At four inches long that does give you some height advantage," says June, "you could probably defeat one in a crisis."

"Well what if there's a gang of them?"

It's all right for you, I think to myself, if a squad of four-inch spiders backs you into a corner you could shoot your way out but such measures are not available to the rest of us. I don't say it, though, for fear of antagonising her.

The report goes straight on to talk about the house centipede with long legs, I've never actually seen a live one, says the curator, but I'd certainly like to. You fucking idiot, I think, some people are just born stupid. Probably if a long-legged house centipede were to appear in here I'd have to call the fire brigade to get rid of it.

But we get to talking a bit better, I suppose she is as much at a loss as me, there is probably no accepted protocol for having a cup of tea with a contract you've decided not to kill after all.

The policemen have cornered the manager in his office at Big Value.

He is frightened and confused, they have shown him some letters purporting to be communications between himself and the manufacturers of soya milk which deal with the deliberate watering down of the product. The manufacturers tell him that they will dilute it and sell it to him cheap and he writes back saying yes, that is fine so long as you offer me a slightly larger cut than you already have. Also among the letters are several from the manager advising some of his suppliers how they can deliver to him cheaply by avoiding paying the correct taxes on the goods.

He has never seen any of the letters before in his life but they bear his signature. The police then play a tape from a wire tap in which the soya milk deal is finalised and the voice on the tape would seem to be unquestionably his.

He cannot understand what is happening. He protests his innocence. They take him down to the station to lay charges.

Muriel is no fool, what's more she is psychic. She realised immediately what has happened, fancy a responsible person like Professor Wing impersonating a council workman just so he could dig up the crown himself. She tells him he ought to be ashamed of himself.

He feels miserable at the prospect of exposure.

"Well this looks like being an all action day," says Chi to the two bodies slumped in front of her.

Julie's hair, normally in occupation of considerable airspace, is huddled round her head. Neither of them can keep their eyes open and, much as they like Chi, they wish she would go away.

"What you need," Chi tells them, "is some fresh air. Let's go for a walk."

They protest feebly but it is no good protesting to someone who used to be the bodyguard of a heroin baron and a short while later they are standing on their doorstep, squinting at the daylight.

"Come on, the walk will do you good," Chi says.

Well that's your opinion, they think, but follow her anyway.

"Where do you want to go?" Chi asks them.

Fran remembers Alby and his desire for a visit. That seems like a reasonable option in the circumstances, at least it's a firm destination where they can sit down and the alternative is probably Chi walking them for miles through some park or something.

"We said we'd visit Alby. Let's go there."

"All right, which direction is it?" Fran and Julie strive to remember.

"This way," they say finally.

Wu is drinking orange juice with his supporters.

"We thought you were going to win."

"I could have won," Wu says, honestly. "But I decided that it was not worth the distress that it would cause Cheng. It was very important to him."

His supporters look at him incredulously. He lost deliberately?

"I don't mind losing. I'm sorry it's upset you though."

The rest of the people at the table look at each other, still incredulous.

Cheng, deliriously happy though he is, does not party quite so uproariously this time because he is working tomorrow and he does not want to be late again. He has to drive his employer down to Brixton to meet some person he has been hunting for. Cheng does not know why his employer is so anxious to see this person, he never tells him anything about his business.

So he celebrated with his friends for a while before going to sleep happy with his victory.

The wife of the manager of Big Value sits in her house doing nothing, the phone rings which is a welcome break, she picks it up and on the other end it is her husband's solicitor telling her not to worry but he has been arrested.

When she asks what for he seems a bit vague, something to do with a conspiracy, he's down at the station now and he's heard through the solicitor's grapevine that the fraud squad have made several arrests at the headquarters of a food firm. But don't worry, he is sure everything will be all right. How very reassuring, she thinks. She arranges to meet the solicitor.

"Why didn't you just report it to your university and get them to recover the crown properly?" asks Muriel.

Professor Wing shifts uncomfortably in his seat and tries to think of an answer, given time he could come up with something reasonable but for the moment he's stumped. Mind you, it is going to have to be a pretty special answer to encompass the theft of the council tools and van as well as the misappropriation of several ancient manuscripts.

"You wanted it all to yourself?" suggests Muriel. "All the credit for its sudden appearance? Maybe see if the magic might work for you? Well, that's understandable I suppose. What are you going to say now?"

This woman certainly asks some awkward questions, thinks the professor. What am I going to say now? If she hadn't recognised me as the workman it would have been no problem.

But then if she hadn't recognised him as the workman he would have found it difficult taking any credit at all for locating it, all he could have said was that someone handed a crown into his department. Now, this woman knew that he had been digging and was fairly seriously in the wrong, but perhaps he could come to some agreement with her which would give him some credit for the discovery?

I'd introduce June to Happy the hamster but I don't expect they'd get on, she probably shoots small creatures for target practice.

I'd have thought she would have gone by now but she's still hanging around. This worries me. What if she changes her mind on ethical grounds? Thanks for the tea Alby, but I've decided I'd better shoot you after all. Also she doesn't like comics or music and I find it hard to talk about anything else. She's not the sort of person you can spout a bit of intellectual philosophy at because, as I discovered previously, she is liable to have read the whole book, furthermore she will quote you large sections from it.

I wonder if she recognises me from any involvement in the anti-milk campaign or if I am just an anonymous person to her. I don't raise this subject but I'm thinking about it, I'm thinking about the Milk Marketing Board, these swines, hire killers to get me would they? I'll pay them back, miserable fuckers, poisoning the country, the stuff is full of strontium 90 you know, it wouldn't surprise me if they inject it straight into the cow.

Cheng reports to work on time.

He is sent on a few errands by his boss, then has to drive him to a meeting, while the meeting is going on Cheng takes the opportunity to hurry to the video shop to buy another game module to practise on.

But he is careless and inside the shop he runs into one of the spectators from the arcade.

"Hello, buying a game to practise on? I didn't know that was allowed . . ."

Cheng curses while at the same time trying to look innocent. He pays for the game and hurries back to the car.

"Brixton," his employer instructs him.

Cheng broods as he drives. He wishes he hadn't been spotted buying that game.

Stacey is finally allowed out of the hospital.

The doctors are plenty annoyed because they still don't know why he got better but they are bored with looking at him so they decide they had better let him go.

"Don't you trouble us again with your phoney illnesses," says the chief consultant as Stacey leaves.

He says goodbye to Pamela Patterson and promises to try and find out why Alby beat her up. She was not seriously hurt as it turned out, but she does have painful bruising and as she lost consciousness when she was hit so the doctors want to keep her under observation for a short while just in case. The experience was highly unpleasant and she is extremely annoyed, you try and sell some comics to someone and what happens? He turns out to be an utter maniac with funny skin who twitches with nerves all through the conversation then attacks you at the first opportunity. Isn't life a riot, she thinks.

"I'm afraid your husband is in serious trouble," says the solicitor. "He seems to have been involved in a major fraud and the police have amassed a large amount of evidence against him."

His wife is distraught, she cannot believe it. Her husband involved in a major fraud? It doesn't sound like him at all, for one thing she would not have supposed him adventurous enough.

"What will happen to him?"

"It depends. Is he a member of the Institute of Directors?"

"I don't think so."

"Hmm. Pity. That might have helped. In that case it may mean prison."

She is kept waiting in the police station for seven hours before they let her see her husband, when she finally does she is shocked by how bad he looks.

"I'm innocent," he tells her. "I've been framed."

Because it is her husband and she knows him inside out, she knows that this is the truth.

This time, thinks the Chinese man as he sits in the back seat on the way to Brixton, I won't have to mess around in the streets. He wonders if he should try to Anglicise himself in his hunt for an aristocratic wife. Would that be better than playing the mysterious oriental? Or how about the hyper-efficient eastern businessman? Decadent playboy? Studious researcher into East-West relations?

He has been secretly buying *Harpers & Queen* magazine to try and pick up some tips but as close study of this magazine reveals neither taste nor intelligence, he realises that he must be reading it incorrectly.

Perhaps he should turn into a complete slob like the aristocrats he sees every night? No, he could never emulate them successfully.

Buses in London are good things to travel on, positively luxurious compared to the tube, a death-trap health hazard if ever I saw one, no chance of coming out alive if a fire starts in a tunnel that's for sure. But they do have dangers of their own. Somebody nasty might sit beside you, they might be fat and crush you into the side, they might be wildly eccentric and try to engage you in conversation. Worst of all is someone sitting beside you when there are whole vacant seats elsewhere on the bus, why is this freak sitting next to me, doesn't he/she know we don't do this sort of thing in this country?

And then there might be someone sitting close by that you don't like the look of, you can't help yourself from glancing their way and they keep catching your eye, why is this person staring at me, you think, and wonder if they're strong enough to beat you up if they suddenly attack you and what if the person has a couple of friends sitting close by just waiting to give someone a good beating?

It's pretty bad hearing someone else's conversation as well, you learn what morons populate the world and this is always depressing.

Tonight I was sitting behind two skinheads, a combination of several of the above dangers, though actually they weren't too bad.

"Why are you doing a bus monologue?" asks June.

"Oh, sorry, was I going on?"

Muriel doesn't feel too unsympathetic to the professor. He wants to go and bury the crown somewhere near to where it was found in the first place and then go and find it again, thereby gaining all the credit. He will, of course, have to bribe the secretary to forget its first appearance.

"After all," he says to Muriel, "it doesn't really matter to you, does it?"

Well, she thinks, if I just told the truth then I'd get the credit for discovering it, which would be something.

But it wouldn't be all that much, she supposes, maybe a small story in a newspaper, someone taking pictures when she really wouldn't have time to hang around because she'd be late for work. And the professor's dishonesty doesn't matter to her, it does not seem to affect her one way or the other. It crosses her mind to ask for something in return but she can't think of anything the professor could give her, or do for her.

"All right," she says. "Take it and bury it. I won't say anything."

She leaves. If she doesn't hurry she'll be late for work.

The car pulls up outside the council estate. The block of flats looks like a borstal. The Chinese man gets out of the car. Cheng steps out with him. They head for the map at the edge of the estate. The correct block identified, they find it and climb the stairs. Cheng knocks on the door.

There's a knock on the door.

I shudder, oh fuck, which enemy is it this time? Which particular evildoer is here for my blood? Or my comics?

"Why don't you answer it?" says June.

Well this person is full of bright suggestions, she doesn't seem to appreciate the constant fear and turmoil that constitute my life. It's all right for her, no one is going to come and molest her lousy plants, but I've got my comics to protect not to mention a personality that seems to antagonise the more violent sort of person.

In fact, all in all, after the dreadful experience of finding my doorstep occupied by a former love affair now heavily armed, I never want to open my door again. So June, helpful soul that she is, goes and answers it for me.

"It's someone to see you," she calls.

What sort of thing is that to say? Of course it's someone to see me or they wouldn't have knocked on my door, would they, that doesn't mean I want to see them. I think of Pamela Patterson possibly arriving with a few friends to pay me back and this makes my heart pound, two people wishing me violence in one day and both appearing at the front door is definitely too much.

"Hello," says a man's voice. I look up and it's the Chinese man who has been hunting me. He is accompanied by his evil-looking bodyguard.

Things are not looking good.

So Muriel goes back to being a nurse and leaves the crown with Professor Wing, he is going to dishonestly discover it again and she is going to gain nothing.

When she reaches the hospital and reports for duty on her ward the first person she sees is Pamela Patterson. Pamela moans because her head is sore where it hit the wall. Poor thing, thinks Muriel, and touches her lightly in sympathy. Immediately Pamela smiles and sits up straight in her bed.

"That's odd," she says, "all of a sudden I feel healthy. In fact I don't think I've ever felt this healthy before."

Muriel is well on her way to becoming a world-famous faith healer.

Wu is teaching some of his supporters to meditate. Once you can meditate, says Wu, then things will seem better. They may not seem wonderful, but definitely better. He has set up an informal class made up of his fans from the arcade.

Wu has discussed the events at the arcade with his teacher. His teacher approves of his actions.

I scream.

It starts involuntarily but I carry it on for a while because it seems like a good thing to do. The dreaded Chinese man has found me, my life starts to flash in front of my eyes, particularly the nasty bits. Oh God a short life and a miserable one, what's he going to kill me with, some fiendish oriental device like the vibrating palm or poisoned bamboo or just an ordinary machine gun, well why is he after me anyway, I mean if he wants to take over my drug dealing that badly he only needed to ask.

"Don't kill me!" I shout.

June.

I'd forgotten about June. On hearing my pitiful wails she rushes back into the room and her entry causes the Chinese man and his hulk-sized bodyguard to look around. I'm not missing my one chance for life, I think, and throw myself at the Chinese man with the intention of killing him on the spot but his bodyguard is too quick for me, he reacts instantaneously, grabbing and holding me.

I wail again. I've seen this in films he's going to snap my spine what an awful way to go I've always been nervous about my spine.

June comes to my rescue. She hits the brute who's holding me. Not bad, I think as he releases me and I crawl for the corner, though I'd have preferred it if she'd shot him. But he's looking puzzled and annoyed and moving towards her so perhaps she still will.

She still doesn't shoot him unfortunately, but she does deliver this appallingly vicious kick and he moans a bit and falls to the floor. From my corner I point at the Chinese man.

"Hit him as well!"

He has his hand in his pocket obviously on the point of drawing out a weapon.

But June, already elevated in my estimation to the mightiest person I have ever met, foils him by whipping out her gun in a dazzlingly fast draw.

"Take your hand out slowly," she says to him.

The Chinese man does as he is told. When his hand emerges it is holding not a gun but a card. I expect it is a deadly throwing weapon, razor sharp at the edges, I've seen *A Touch of Zen* too you know.

But June takes the card and her hand doesn't start bleeding, she passes it to me as I emerge slightly from the corner, it seems to be an ordinary business card. It reads W. PETERS, IMPORT EXPORT. I have difficulty believing that this son of Fu Man Chu is really called W. Peters.

"Why have you been trying to kill me?" I ask him aggressively.

He pretends to look puzzled. "I have not been trying to kill you."

"You've been following me around and asking my friends where you could find me."

"But only to repay a debt of honour. You are Alby Starvation, yes? Well your diet cure saved my life. I was a sick man until I stopped drinking milk."

June looks at me. I look at her.

We all look at the bodyguard lying unconscious on the floor.

The manager of Big Value is going to be charged with serious fraud.

He has been remanded in custody in the meantime because at the preliminary hearing the police recommended that he should not be released on bail as such an organised racketeer was bound to have many criminal accomplices who would help him leave the country before trial.

So his wife visits him and then goes home and does not know what to do. The case against him is cast iron. He is going to be jailed for a long time. She wonders what she will do.

As a first move she decides to wallpaper the house with some paper that she likes.

I am feeling hard done by.

"Well for fuck's sake," I say, "how was I to know that was why they was here?"

June looks unconvinced. She is ministering to the bodyguard who has now recovered sufficiently to whimper a little. I guess she is annoyed at being involved unnecessarily in this violence, well I don't think it was my fault, how was I meant to know he only wanted to thank me for curing him, this whole milk business has been one long pain, I wish the stuff had never been invented. Any cow that crosses my path in the future better be careful.

I'm saved from further remonstrations by another knock on the door.

I've no enthusiasm for visitors but at least this one should be fairly safe as I seem to have accounted for all of my potential killers for the time being.

So I open the door and it's Fran and Julie and a woman I recognise as Chi, their kung fu teacher. Fran and Julie look terrible, I wonder if I should make some excuse and send them away to avoid explaining the scenes of violence in my living room but I really cannot be bothered.

Besides, they look like they are too sick to notice the body. "Hello Alby Starvation, friend of all hamsters," says Fran. "Is your toilet free?" She hurries past.

Julie and Chi follow me into the living room.

As soon as Chi and W. Peters see each other they scream and rush at each other, engaging immediately in a frighteningly violent kung fu battle. This sort of thing seems to be normal these days in this house. Those of us not engaged in fighting look bemused and retreat to the walls for safety. What the fuck is going on?

Pamela Patterson leaves the hospital, the doctors don't mind too much about her quick recovery as she was suffering from a common complaint, being beaten up, and not from a mystery illness. If she wants to recover too quickly from being beaten up then that's her business.

As she leaves the hospital grounds she checks in her bag to make sure she still has the slip of paper that Stacey gave her on which he has written Alby's address.

She waits at the bus stop.

"Why are these people trying to kill each other?" yells June to me over the noise of the battle. We are huddled behind a chair.

"I really don't know," I tell her honestly. Julie is beside us and she doesn't know either.

Fran appears in the doorway, she halts in surprise as Chi's body flies past her to land nimbly in a fighting stance. Both the Chinese man and Chi would appear to be masters of the fighting arts, what's more they seem to be evenly matched. They face each other in silence.

Normally I'd be quite happy to let them get on with it but it is my living room and I'm worried that Happy's house and also Happy himself might be demolished by a stray kick, so I try and inject some rationality into the proceedings.

"Why are you fighting?"

Neither of them look at me but Chi answers from her motionless stance.

"He stole our money and left me for dead in Cambodia."

"Well, what interesting lives some people do have. I never knew you were in Cambodia."

My attempts at conversation get nowhere however, and they start fighting again.

"Can't you stop them?" I say to June.

She shakes her head.

I can't really blame her for not wanting to get involved, the result of her last action is still lying on the couch. Fran has joined Julie on the floor in the far corner of the room and they would appear to be going to sleep.

There is another lull in the combat during which the Chinese man, who I am still having difficulty believing is really called W. Peters, denies running out on Chi and says that she was on the point of double-crossing him and turning him in to the authorities in return for her own freedom. Not unnaturally she denies this and they start fighting again. This violence is starting to make me feel pretty ill, both of them are shouting and yelling, I don't know if they frighten each other but they certainly frighten me.

There's yet another knock on the door. I hope that it's the police or the army come to stop the noise, though now I think about it if the police arrive and search this flat then I am going to be in some difficulties, anyway I risk life and limb fleeing the room into the hall and when I open the door it's my friend Stacey.

"You're better!" I cry.

Last reports of Stacey had him dying in the hospital and it sure is good news to find him living on my doorstep.

"What's going on?" he asks me as a particularly piercing yell flies past from the other room.

"I don't know. Two complete strangers are having a fight in my living room. When did you get better?"

"Just yesterday." He tells me about his miracle cure. "Why did you beat up that girl?"

The manager's wife is called Jez. She is busy papering the walls, listening to the news on the radio, there is a big strike in the North Sea oilfields where the divers dispute has spread, she knows all about it already because she has heard several news bulletins on the same subject this morning.

She is papering on her own, a difficult task, but she feels good when it goes well and this compensates for the disasters.

She looks out of her window and she sees a young woman standing at the bus stop outside. The woman's attention has wandered from waiting for a bus and is now focussed on trying to wrench a large wooden stave out of the garden fence.

Why is she trying to wreck my fence, thinks Jez and goes to the door to find out.

"Why are you trying to wreck my fence?"

The woman halts in her efforts. "I'm sorry," she says to Jez, "I'm on my way to see this man who beat me up and I wanted this as a weapon."

"Oh, that's all right in that case. Take as many staves as you want."

"Thank you. Why are you covered in paste?"

"I'm wallpapering, I've never done it before, it's hard on your own."

"I know how to wallpaper, it's not too difficult once you get the hang of it."

"Well perhaps after you have seen this man you could come and help me as payment for the stave from my fence?"

"Yes," says Pamela Patterson, "I will."

A bus lumbers onto the horizon and she hurries back to the bus stop. She clutches the large piece of wood.

I can't imagine how Stacey knows about me attacking that girl. Perhaps my face is up on wanted posters all over town. But he heads towards the noise, naturally curious, before I can question him further.

The room is a bit crowded now, what with me, Fran, Julie, Stacey, Chi, the Chinese man, and his bodyguard all struggling for space. The fight continues in difficult circumstances. We watch their magical technique. Chi flies into the attack with an open-handed strike to the eyes but the Chinese man retreats diagonally and counter-attacks in the same instant, forcing Chi back.

This looks like it may go on for some time. Have you ever had strangers fighting in your house? It's not too pleasant, but because there does not seem to be anyone after me at the present and the most pressing threats against me have disappeared, I'm feeling fairly mellow.

"Why don't you pack it in and give us a rest?" shouts Fran, briefly opening her eyes. Julie nods agreement though she respects her kung fu teacher too much to shout at her.

The combatants come to a reluctant halt. We all look at each other. Suddenly my flat is a meeting place for all sorts of exotic people, big criminals, drug dealers, hired killers, I'm not sure if Fran and Julie count as exotic but they're certainly quite unusual. Stacey's a bit on the ordinary side I suppose.

Me, I'm a hero. Well in my own mind I am anyway.

There is another knock on the door.

Nothing will surprise me this time, I expect it's the head of the New York mafia or the Argentinian Ambassador dropping in for a chat. I wait for one of the assembled throng to answer it because I seem to have spent the entire day opening the door and each time I do something unpleasant happens, excepting Stacey of course, his recovery is good news so long as he keeps his thieving hands off my comics. I notice Fran and Julie talking to the hamster, he's probably asking who all these people are and have they brought him any biscuits?

No one does open the door but it doesn't matter because I obviously didn't shut it properly the last time and there are footsteps in the hall. A face appears in the door.

Fucking hell, it's Pamela Patterson.

She advances into the room with a mean look, I hate people giving me mean looks but I could probably cope with it except I see she is carrying a great big stick. Thinking quickly I retreat behind June.

"I was dropped on my head as a baby," I blurt.

Pamela doesn't look sympathetic and keeps advancing.

"You'd better keep away, I've got plenty of heavy connections you know."

"Like who?" says June, very unhelpfully.

"Well there's Jock and Sanny down the road. They're quite tough." I manoeuvre myself further behind her.

"Are you still interested in selling the comics?"

I catch sight of myself in the mirror. I'm not looking too good, I think.